A MESSAGE TO THE
Glorious Church

VOLUME I

A Verse by Verse Study of
Ephesians Chapters 1-4

RICK JOYNER

MorningStar Publications
A DIVISION OF MORNINGSTAR FELLOWSHIP CHURCH
P.O. Box 440
Wilkesboro, NC 28697

A Message to the Glorious Church, Volume I
Rick Joyner
Copyright © 2003
Second Printing 2004

International Standard Book Number—1-929371-29-2

All Scripture quotations are taken from the New American Standard Version unless otherwise indicated, copyright (c) 1983 by Thomas Nelson, Inc.

Table of Contents

Part IV: Built for Eternity • 111

Part V: A More Solid Foundation • 159

Preface

Paul's Epistle to the Ephesians is considered by many to be the most extraordinary, interesting, and powerful book in the Bible. While that may be debatable, the fact that it contains the most clear and detailed account of what individual Christians and the church as a whole are called to be, is not debatable. There is simply no other book in the Bible that comes close to Ephesians in this matter.

This is Volume I of a verse by verse study of the book of Ephesians, which concludes at the end of Chapter Four. This Epistle has three main themes and several other minor ones, which could have each been a complete study. Even so, I felt that it should be combined into just two volumes so that there would be a strong bridge between the two.

Even though this is a verse by verse study of Ephesians, I do not consider this to be an in-depth study of the Epistle. There are numerous individual verses in Ephesians that are worthy of an entire book. In fact, I did write an entire book on just one of those verses entitled, *The Surpassing Greatness of His Power,* and I still felt that it was handled superficially when it was finished. This is certainly a great glory of the Word of God—there seems to be no end to the depths of revelation and knowledge that can be mined from it.

I know that those who would pick up a book like this are already true spiritual treasure hunters. Ephesians is the source of many of the greatest treasures that I have ever found in the Bible, but more than just conveying these to you, I pray that you do not settle for them, but are inspired to go even deeper into studying this great and expansive Epistle of vision and hope. However, our primary goal is not just to find the treasures, but to cash in on them! By this I mean that the treasures do not just inspire us, but we want to walk in them.

Someone is going to walk in everything that Paul saw the glorious church becoming. Why not us? Regardless of your present condition, there is nothing keeping you from becoming the person who will walk closer to God than anyone else, with the exception of the Son of God Himself. There are no limitations put on anyone in pursuit of our full purpose in Him. We are only limited by our own faith and patience, which in Christ also relates to our discipline.

Overall, it seems that there has been a meltdown of faithfulness in the church over the last few decades, especially in the Western church. This has been happening to such a degree that some have called it "the great falling away," and others the time when "the love of most will grow cold." This may be true, overall, but in the midst of this time there is something very encouraging happening. There are an increasing number of individuals who are resolving to walk in their full purpose in Christ. These have counted the cost, and are willing to pay any price. They are sacrificing all worldly ambitions and dreams, and enduring any hardship, to know and walk with God. As the times make this more and more difficult, this makes these faithful ones even greater treasures to God.

This is your reason for being on the earth. You are not here just to find treasure, but to be a treasure to God. What makes something a treasure is that it is either rare or hard to find. This is true of the great souls for which Ephesians was especially written. It is right that we lament for those who backslide and fall away from the faith, but for those who have the true faith, their encouragement does not come from what other people do. Our encouragement to keep going comes from the knowledge that if we spent our entire lives to bring our King pleasure for just a single moment, it would have been a life of such glorious success that no amount of earthly treasure could ever compare to it.

Ultimately, our success in Christ comes down to this—not the blessings that we have received or what we have gained, but the blessing that we have been to the King. We all start by looking for treasures, and for those who pursue the true treasures of the Spirit, it is sometimes a very lonely pursuit. Even so, there is a point at which we must rise to an even higher goal of being the treasure. There is a point when our vision must be fulfilled and we attain to what we have seen. That is our quest. As we are told in Ephesians 4:15, this is nothing less than the fact that **"we are to grow up in all aspects into Him who is the head, even Christ."**

PART I

A Vision of the Glorious Quest

A Study of Ephesians Chapter 1

CHAPTER ONE

Climbing the Mountain

The Christian life is the ultimate quest and the greatest adventure that we can experience in this life. The most noble cause and the greatest purpose that anyone can have is to serve the King of kings. Every Christian has a calling that is higher than any earthly office or position. This book is a study of how every Christian can walk in this glorious purpose, as outlined in one of the most extraordinary books of the New Testament, Paul's Epistle to the Ephesians.

I have been told many times that it was the revelation of the magnificence of the Christian life that made *The Final Quest* so popular. I confess that the message contained in that book radically changed my own life and message. However, the purpose of the visions that I wrote about were not to just make an interesting book, but to compel Christians to take up the cause, pursue the quest—to actually live the adventure. The book that is now in your hands is for those who are committed to turning dreams into reality, and visions into goals that can ultimately be accomplished.

I climbed a mountain in the visions I wrote about in *The Final Quest*. It was a majestic, extraordinary mountain. It was not easy to climb, but it was crowned with glory. This mountain represented the Scriptures, the Word of God. The most noble cause and the most lofty thoughts that have ever been comprehended by man are found in the Bible. The pursuit of understanding the ways of God which are found in the Bible is an adventure in itself, and is like no other. The Bible is the map that was given to guide our lives—but the goal is life. The adventure is real.

There were different levels on the mountain that I saw which represented different biblical truths. It was by understanding the truth on one level that enabled me to climb to the next level. A fundamental message of that vision is the systematic ascent which the Christian life is intended to be. Our ascent is based on a systematic understanding of the truth of God that is revealed in the Scriptures and translates into a nature that becomes more and more like the King's nature. With that changed nature comes more faith and more authority to do greater and greater exploits in His name. This book is a practical, step-by-step pursuit of an ascending Christian life which is outlined in the book of Ephesians.

For us to benefit from the truth of this message we must understand that the primary reason for the circumstances that the Lord allows in our lives, and a primary reason why He allows us to suffer the attacks of the enemy, is to compel us to go higher up that mountain of spiritual maturity. We are going to study the book of Ephesians in some depth. It is a very practical road map up that mountain, written by one of the greatest saints who ever lived—the apostle Paul.

In this verse by verse study of Ephesians, we will gain a clear and expansive vision of what we are called to be in Christ, both as a church and as individuals. Although this Epistle is like a map for climbing the mountain, it also contains a compass that points directly to the peak. It gives us practical understanding of the next step, while capturing our hearts with a passion for reaching the top. This Epistle gives some of the greatest encouragement in the Bible for why such a quest is the greatest human adventure that can be had on the earth.

Therefore, my prayer for all who read this is to be likewise encouraged and challenged to continually go higher in the Lord. Our goal is nothing less than to be like Him and do the works that He did, to the glory of His name. We can be sure that as we approach the end of this age there will be a church that climbs this mountain and stands triumphantly at the top. Then the whole world will stand in awe and marvel at the demonstration of what God created man to be.

As I climbed that mountain in **The Final Quest,** it took a supreme effort. Not only did it require concentration to watch every step, but I also had to fight the enemy at the same time. I can still vividly remember the elation and relief as I reached every new level. There was room to rest a bit and regain my strength. However, the best part was that at each new level I received a clear view of my position and the battle that was raging all around me on the mountain.

With each level there was greater vision and understanding. I can still vividly remember how encouraging it was when I reached a new level and saw the path going on farther up the mountain. There was a drawing to the top that was greater than any desire for rest or peace. Just seeing the way to go a little higher would energize me and give me courage even in the worst of the battle. I still think that this is one thing that helps Christians to endure and prevail in the battles of life more than anything else—we must have a vision for going higher. Possibly more than any other book in the Bible, the book of Ephesians is the light on the path to go higher regardless of the level that we are now on.

Even though there was a deep beckoning in my heart to keep going higher on the mountain, I also knew I needed to stay at each level I attained until I had the sense that I had really been established there. In some ways the ascent was painfully slow, and I needed to stay at certain plateaus longer than others. In the vision, I saw many who tried to race to the top, but none of them made it. As badly as I wanted to keep going up, my goal was not speed, but a sure footing that would enable me to make it to the top, not just go a little higher. That should be our devotion in all spiritual growth. We must proceed higher and higher, but we must also do it from a rock solid foundation. As we are told in Hebrews 6:11-12:

And we desire that each one of you show the same diligence to the full assurance of hope until the end,

that you do not become sluggish, but imitate those who through faith and patience inherit the promises (NKJV).

It takes "faith *and* patience to inherit the promises." Have you ever wondered why we have such a large "Faith Movement?" And at the same time, have you even heard of a "Patience Movement?" Therefore, my prayer for those who read this book is from the two verses above, that you:

1) Grow in diligence so that you do not become **"sluggish"** in your walk,

2) grow in the **"full assurance of hope"** that will keep you to the end,

3) grow in both **"faith and patience"** so that you will **"inherit the promises,"**

4) and that your victory becomes so visible to others that it compels them to want to make the same quest.

Again, we must have the vision of ascending in our walk with the Lord, but the height of our ascent will depend on the strength of our foundation. I am continually alarmed by two things that I see in many believers. The first is that those who tend to have a strong foundation for their beliefs usually do not have a vision for going higher. Their vision is simply a strong foundation and they have little sense of what it is that God intended to be built on that foundation. The second great alarm is that those who have a vision for going higher usually have a weak foundation because they were too impatient to lay a strong one. We must combine our faith and vision with the patience to plant our feet on the most solid ground as we ascend. Those who have a foundation without vision will stagnate. Those with vision but without a devotion to the Scriptures and sound teaching, will only become more dangerous the higher they go.

So we must learn to continually strengthen our foundation, as well as go higher in both vision and spiritual attainment. Until we are like the Lord in character, which is the fruit of the Spirit, we have not yet attained our purpose on this earth. If we are not doing the works that He did, which is the effective use of the ministries and gifts of the Spirit, we have not yet attained the maturity and fruitfulness to which we are called.

This book is broken down necessarily into short chapters for each verse of Ephesians. As every student of the Bible learns quickly, the Bible is full of redundancies and repetitions. This is by Divine intent. Some studies have indicated that fewer than ten percent of people can retain a new thought the first time they hear it, and most people need to hear something at least four times in order to retain it. Our goal as Christians must be to go even further than just comprehension and retention of the truth—the truth must be transformed into our nature.

As the Lord made clear, it is not those who just hear the Word who are building their houses on the rock, but those who are hearing and obeying. We do want to hear His Word and understand it, but we must also realize that this is just the beginning—we must be doers of His Word.

Those who have true faith in the Word of God are not just those who believe that everything which happened in the Bible really happened. That is important, but by itself is not enough. One who has true faith in the Bible will have faith to see the same things that were done in the Bible, also done in their own lives. The Word of God is living! It is now. As the Scripture states that the Lord quoted when being tempted by the devil: **"It is written, "Man shall not live on bread alone, but on every word that proceeds out of the mouth of God"" (Matthew 4:4).** Note that this is every word that *"proceeds* out of the mouth of God,"** not every word that *proceeded.* The Word of God which we live on is that which He is saying to us now, in the present.

Those who accomplish the greatest things with their lives are always people of vision—but vision alone is not enough. Those who have the greatest visions will not, by that alone, be the ones who will be the greatest heroes in heaven. One who accomplishes a lesser vision will be greater than the one who had a great vision but did not accomplish it. Our vision of higher ground will only lead to failure in our faith if we do not also have the continual reinforcement of the practical teachings of the faith so as to accomplish it.

As we climb the mountain of God's truth, the desire for personal recognition and reward will only carry us a little way. If we would be honest, that is probably what motivates anyone to get going, but that alone is too shallow to sustain us through the battles which will surely come. As I climbed that mountain in the visions, I could only see a level or two above me, and sometimes could not even see anyone above. The higher you go up the mountain, the fewer people you will see, and the fewer who will see you. However, by this time the few glimpses of the glory above should be more than enough to keep us going.

As we begin to more fully behold the unfathomable glory of the Lord, to seek any kind of personal recognition that would distract from having others look to Him becomes increasingly profane. Who could ever presume glory or recognition in His presence? If we are still in pursuit of our own glory or recognition, it is a good indication of just what a low level of spiritual maturity we are still at.

Even so, there may be no greater fulfillment than hearing those words from our King on the great Judgment Day: **"Well done good and faithful servant!" (Matthew 25:21 NIV)** There is nothing more fulfilling than growing spiritually, going higher and higher. As we grow spiritually, we become less self-centered and more Christ-centered. In the end, our greatest fulfillment will not come from the recognition that we may receive, but from whatever recognition we were able to bring to the King and His message in this life.

Once we see His glory, we will become so addicted to it that we will endure any struggle and fight any battle, just to get closer. As we behold His glory we will also be changed by it and start to see as He sees, feel what He feels, and think what He thinks. The

Lord's heart is still for the lost—those who are still captives of the devil and doing his will. So as we go higher into His glory there will also arise a compelling desire to go back and help others get free and begin their own quest to climb the mountain. Because of this, we learn that there are times to climb and go higher, and there are times to go back to help others.

However, the higher we have gone, and the more glory we have beheld and been changed by, the more we will be able to help those who are still in darkness. This is what I believe Jacob saw when he beheld the ladder into heaven. The angels (or messengers) of God were both ascending and descending. Jesus also referred to this ladder concerning Himself when He told Nathaniel in John 1:51, **"Truly, truly, I say to you, you will see the heavens opened and the angels of God ascending and descending on the Son of Man."** Jesus is Jacob's ladder which we ascend and descend upon.

It may seem a paradox at times, but it is our calling in Christ to both go higher and go lower. We are called to ascend into the heavenly places and be seated with Him there, and at the same time descend to the earth with the evidence of heaven's reality. As children of the King, we are members of the greatest aristocracy in the universe, yet we go to the lowest sinners as their servants to help them join the true nobility.

In the visions that I wrote about in *The Final Quest*, I also learned that the more glory I beheld and was changed by, the more I needed to wear a cloak of humility that hid it. That too may seem to be a paradox, but there is a higher wisdom that we must have as we experience the glory of God. This is the wisdom that will enable us to use the glory to enlighten people without blinding them. When someone has been in darkness for a very long time, even a little light can cause them to withdraw in pain. We want to always use just enough to draw them, helping them to gradually open their eyes to more and more light.

The glory is meant to change us from the inside out, and the glory is hidden so that it only comes out through our words and actions. Therefore, those who have the most true glory of the

Lord will wear the most humble clothing. Those who have seen His glory are appalled at the very idea of trying to draw attention to themselves. These live to see the name of the Lord glorified— not to draw attention to themselves. Those who have seen His glory know that even the greatest glory that we could attain to in this iife will fade in His presence like the stars when the sun rises.

In my visions, the ledges on the mountain that represented the higher truths became increasingly narrow and precarious. One could not safely climb the higher part of the mountain without having the surest footing. Our goal should be to go higher, while at the same time making our standing even more sure. Therefore, the vision we seek will always be embedded securely in a constant examination, reviewing, and honoring of the basic precepts of the faith.

I have personally watched many fall off the mountain in my visions and in real life. Those who fall are inevitably those who try to go higher while becoming arrogant toward the basics. There is more depth of wisdom and understanding in even the most basic Christian truths than probably anyone has yet been able to fully comprehend. The examination of the basic truths in increasing depth is one way that we can go higher. I learned this in the visions where some of the doors that no one wanted to go through, which seemed to go lower, were actually short cuts to the top.

Digging deeper into the basics of faith can be a mine that always leads to the mother lode of wisdom which can never be exhausted. Each one contains unfathomable treasure which could capture our interest for many, many years. I therefore have learned to appreciate those who park for a time at any level of the mountain to mine the treasures there. These provide a continual enrichment of faith that we all benefit from. We must never become arrogant toward those who may seem to be at a lower level—they may be far deeper than we are, and equipped to go far higher in a shorter period of time when they do begin to climb.

I know that my own calling is mostly to those who are in the climbing process. Those are the ones who will primarily be drawn to this kind of book. Because of this, I pray that by reading this book, you are compelled to climb with wisdom and humility, and appreciate the constant reminders of the basics of faith which we must have to be successful in our climb. Many of these reminders and repetitions are embedded in this book, just as I believe we find in them in the Scriptures. We continually need the calling to go higher, and the reminders are our foundations. Few seem to be able to do both, but we must.

I look forward to meeting you at the top. Let us resolve together that even if we slip and fall, and even if we suffer wounds and setbacks, we will keep getting up and keep reaching higher, until we stand victorious before His glory.

C H A P T E R   T W O

A Map to the Kingdom

There are a number of Scriptures which illuminate a progressive walk and maturity in the Lord, as in II Peter 1:2-7:

> **Grace and peace be multiplied to you in the knowledge of God and of Jesus our Lord,**

> **as His divine power has given to us all things that pertain to life and godliness, through the knowledge of Him who called us by glory and virtue,**

> **by which have been given to us exceedingly great and precious promises, that through these you may be partakers of the divine nature, having escaped the corruption that is in the world through lust.**

> **But also for this very reason, giving all diligence, add to your faith virtue, to virtue knowledge,**

> **to knowledge self-control, to self-control perseverance, to perseverance godliness,**

> **to godliness brotherly kindness, and to brotherly kindness love (NKJV).**

One reason why many Christians live in defeat and frustration is that when they receive a vision of the top of the mountain, they try to go straight there without learning to climb step-by-step. The zeal of those who want to go straight to the top is admirable, but the Christian walk is practical. When we are born again all things become new, but then we must go through the process of having our minds renewed. Our goal for this study is to follow a plan that produces measurable progress.

As we are told in I Timothy 1:5: **"But the goal of our instruction is love from a pure heart and a good conscience and a sincere faith."** In the King James Version, the last part of this verse is translated, **"a faith unfeigned."** Basically our goal should be to have **"love from a pure heart,"** and consistent, unwavering faith. The goal is the top of the mountain, but how do we get there? From the verses quoted above in II Peter, we can deduce that it will come by the following process:

1) *Grace and peace are multiplied to us as we grow in the knowledge of God and His Son, Jesus Christ.* Our first goal should be to learn about the Lord—to know His ways, not just His acts.

2) *It is His divine power that has already granted to us everything we need through the knowledge of Him.* We must learn to live by His power, not our own strength, and this too we come to through knowing Him.

3) *Through Him we are given exceedingly great and precious promises and through these we will partake of His divine nature.* The greatest promise of all is that our fellowship with God has been restored, and as we draw near to Him, we behold His glory which will change us into His same image.

4) *He enables us to escape the corruption that is in the world through lust.* The Law demonstrated how futile it is to focus on the lust to get free of it—we get free from the lust of the world by being captured by the glory of the Lord.

5) *For this reason we should give all diligence to add to our faith:*
virtue,
to virtue, knowledge,
to knowledge, self-control,
to self-control, perseverance,
to perseverance, godliness,
to godliness, brotherly kindness,
and to brotherly kindness, love.

It is obvious how each of these qualities builds upon the previous one. These are the seven basic levels of the mountain that I was shown in my visions. There are many aspects contained in each of these. For example, with levels of knowledge, there are many deep mines of truth. On the level of godliness there was also included the power gifts of the Spirit. As I was told, we cannot be like God without power, and we cannot be witnesses of the Almighty without power. Even so, the ultimate goal and highest level is love.

We are then told in II Peter 1:8-11:

For if these things are yours and abound, you will be neither barren nor unfruitful in the knowledge of our Lord Jesus Christ.

For he who lacks these things is shortsighted, even to blindness, and has forgotten that he was cleansed from his old sins.

Therefore, brethren, be even more diligent to make your call and election sure, for if you do these things you will never stumble;

for so an entrance will be supplied to you abundantly into the everlasting kingdom of our Lord and Savior Jesus Christ (NKJV).

Our goal is to live fully, every day, in every place, in the kingdom of God by abiding in the King Himself. If we do this, we will be like Him in nature, and be used by Him to do the works that He wants us to do. We want to take every thought captive and make it obedient to Him. We want to think as He thinks, and to speak what He wants us to speak. We want to see everyone as He does, hear them as He does, and understand them as He does, so that we touch their lives the way He wants to touch them through us. We want to walk in the love of God with His power flowing through us to demonstrate that love.

As growing in the characteristics listed in II Peter 1 is the way the entrance into the kingdom of God is "abundantly" supplied to us, each of these is worthy of considering in greater depth. We will do this beginning with the next chapter.

C H A P T E R   T H R E E

A Vision of
Full Purpose

Since this study is based on the book of Ephesus, and Ephesus means "full purpose," this fundamental precept must be kept foremost in our hearts. Our goal is not to just do some things for the Lord—our goal must be to walk in our full purpose for which it says we were foreknown before the foundation of the world. The book of Ephesians is a call to those who live for the highest pursuit, which is the most noble cause—serving the King of kings. This is what you must set in your heart right now, that you were bought with a price and you are no longer your own— you have been called into the highest purpose of all upon the earth—you are in the service of the King.

It is noteworthy that it was a letter to the church in Ephesus which was the format for Paul to articulate the glorious vision of the purpose of the church. Ephesus was one of the most strategic cities in the first century for both the Roman Empire and the church. It was no accident that this city was also the center of worship for the goddess, Diana, which represents a satanic counterpart to what the church is called to be. It is a general principle that the major strongholds over regions and cities usu- ally are a direct counter to God's purpose in that city or region.

It also seems fitting that the Lord should begin His message to the seven churches in Asia with the extraordinary church at Ephesus. We will therefore do a general study of both the Lord's message to Ephesus, and the other biblical references to this city in order to gain a better understanding of the setting for these messages.

The first mention of Ephesus in Acts 18 seems to indicate anything but a significant beginning to the great spiritual history of this city. While on a missionary journey Paul stopped in Ephesus, and as was his custom, began to reason with the Jews in the synagogue. They asked him to stay longer, but he refused so that he could keep the feast in Jerusalem. It seemed that Paul just turned his back on an open door to share the gospel, but he must have sensed that its time was not full yet.

Later Paul passed back through Ephesus and found some disciples there who had only been acquainted with John's baptism. Paul taught them about the baptism of the Holy Spirit, and prayed for them to receive it, which they did. This led Paul to stay longer, so that he ended up teaching for two years in the school of Tyrannus. This must have been one of the most extraordinary schools in history. Not only did the Lord begin to do "extraordinary miracles" through Paul, but "... **all who dwelt in Asia heard the word of the Lord Jesus, both Jews and Greeks" (Acts 19:10).** What a class that must have been!

We may wonder how such a thing could have happened— for all of Asia to hear the word of the Lord because Paul teaches in a school for two years. But there are spiritually strategic places which have "spiritual amplifiers" or "spiritual megaphones." Things that happen in such places will be spread abroad. Some of these places have this permanently, such as Jerusalem, and others such as Antioch and Ephesus seemed to have had this anointing for just a period of time. We can also see when this is beginning to happen to a place, Satan will always try to use it for his own purposes, just as he did at Ephesus with the goddess, Diana, intending to spread the worship of her all over the world.

Of course, the enemy will try to preempt and counterfeit everything that the Lord is doing in every place. The Lord allows this for His own purposes. The conflict between the two will highlight the contrasts, and work to strengthen that which is real. If the Lord had wanted us to grow without conflict, He could have bound Satan immediately after His resurrection, and established His kingdom over the world right then. This whole church age is for our sake—it is training for reigning. The Lord does not mean for it to be easy.

Another lesson we see with Ephesus is that this most significant church had a most inconspicuous and seemingly insignificant beginning. The majority of the great works of God throughout history have had the most humble beginnings. For this reason even Jesus was born in a stable, so that the only way He could be found was by revelation.

Arguably the greatest Christian movement since the first century, as far as numbers of people who were touched, was the Pentecostal renewal; and it began with a handful of the very poorest people who owned almost nothing but a desire for God. They wanted Him more than they wanted oxygen, and that tiny little group started a spiritual fire that still burns around the world, touching millions and millions more every year. One of the first tests of those who would be used to do significant things is to be faithful with the little, seemingly insignificant things.

The little group of disciples that Paul ran across at Ephesus was in one way a very sad thing, and in another way it was very encouraging. It was sad that they were still only acquainted with John's baptism. John was a forerunner. He came to point the way to Jesus, but these had obviously spent many years not knowing that the one John had come to prepare the way for had also come and gone. Throughout church history we find many similar groups who get caught up in the excitement of the forerunner movements, but fail to make the jump to the movements for which these came to prepare the way.

The encouraging thing about these disciples was that they had remained so faithful for so long with so little. The period of time between John's baptism and Paul's visit was nearly twenty years. Today it is hard to get people to wait twenty weeks for what the Lord has promised. Because of the faithfulness of these few who had so little to stand with, the Lord sent them one of His greatest apostles to lead them to the fulfillment of what John's ministry had prepared them for. These twelve faithful ones became a foundation that something very significant would be built upon.

In my thirty years of ministry I have watched many of those who seemingly had the most potential end up living lives of frustration, bitterness, and failure, because they were lacking just one thing—patience. If we let impatience drive us, we will miss our purpose in the Lord. Impatience is not a fruit of the Spirit, and the Spirit will never lead us if we allow impatience to control our actions. If we are faithful with what we have been given, we can count on one thing that is as sure as the sun rising—the Lord will not forget us.

One principle to consider—the longer and harder it is to enter into the fulfillment of your promises, the more significant they probably are. The easier and more quickly your promises are fulfilled, the more insignificant they probably are.

CHAPTER FOUR

Predestined for a Purpose

As we continue our study on our full purpose in Christ, we will examine verse by verse the depth of this revelation found in the book of Ephesians. In Chapter 1:1 we read:

Paul, an apostle of Jesus Christ by the will of God, to the saints who are in Ephesus, and faithful in Christ Jesus (NKJV).

This is a letter from the apostle **"to the saints who are in Ephesus,"** and the **"faithful in Christ Jesus."** Even though we may not be from Ephesus, Paul also addresses this letter to the **"faithful in Christ Jesus."** This letter is especially to the faithful in Christ throughout every generation. That also is our primary calling—to be faithful to Christ in all things.

In the next verse Paul continues with:

Grace to you and peace from God our Father and the Lord Jesus Christ.

This is no insignificant salutation. Paul begins by releasing grace and peace from the Father and the Lord Jesus. There is no force on earth that can overpower the grace of God, and no force that we cannot overcome if we will abide in the peace of God. This is the ultimate blessing, and Paul would not just casually write this most powerful greeting. We may also deduce from these words that this is what the letter is intended to impart into our life.

We must also understand that it is essential for us to understand both the grace and peace of God as we begin to perceive the high calling of God that we have been given. The grace of God is given to the humble (see James 4:6), and the peace of God is the result of walking in righteousness and obedience to Him (see Romans 14:17). We will study these in more depth later, but for now let us grasp that it is primary to our calling that we seek and walk in the grace and peace of God every day.

Then Paul proceeds with another bombshell in verse 3:

Blessed be the God and Father of our Lord Jesus Christ, who has blessed us with every spiritual blessing in the heavenly places in Christ

We have been blessed **"with every spiritual blessing."** We could dwell on this alone for many days. We do need to understand the spiritual blessings that we have received, and this is a basic theme that Paul develops throughout the rest of this Epistle, which we too will examine. For now let us understand that there is not a single spiritual blessing that has not been given to us. The least of the spiritual blessings are greater than the greatest of the natural blessings and natural treasures that can be found on the earth. The inheritance of every Christian is far beyond any comprehension of the earthly. One of the reasons why we are going to search this book in depth is to discover what it is that has been freely made available to us in Christ, which we can begin to walk in right now!

As he also makes clear, these spiritual blessings are in **"the heavenly places in Christ."** When we are born again we become a new creation, or literally, a new species. We are a species that bridges the realities of the heavenly and earthly realms. We should actually be more at home in the heavenly realm than in the earthly. As we are told in II Corinthians 5:5-7:

Now He who has prepared us for this very thing is God, who also has given us the Spirit as a guarantee.

**So we are always confident, knowing that while we
are at home in the body we are absent from the Lord.**

For we walk by faith, not by sight (NKJV).

This too must be comprehended from the beginning.
There is a saying that some people are "so heavenly minded
that they are no earthly good." This may be true in some cases,
but it is much better to be that way than to be so earthly minded
that you do not walk in the Spirit, which is in fact the case with
many. Our calling is heavenly, and those who are truly heavenly
minded are the ones who have consistently done the most good
on earth too.

It should be the nature of every Christian to be more at
home in the spiritual realm than in the earthly. The fact is that
probably very few Christians are at home at all in the spiritual
realm, but actually are afraid of spiritual things and spiritual
people. This will change before the end of this age, as many
biblical prophecies testify, and we would do well right now to
begin seeking to understand the nature of our spiritual calling,
and all of the spiritual blessings that we have been given here.
The greatest of all that is upon the earth is not equal to the least
of that which is in heaven. Only the most spiritually blind and
foolish are overly concerned about their earthly inheritance. This
is another theme that is expanded on in this letter, and we will
examine it more fully. For now, let us go on to verse four:

**...just as He chose us in Him before the foundation
of the world, that we should be holy and without blame
before Him in love (NKJV)**

Each one of us was known by Him and chosen in Him
"before the foundation of the world." As incomprehensible
as this is to our finite minds, He could see the end before the
beginning, and He knew us before we existed. He knew us and
chose us to walk before Him holy, without blame, and in love.

If we are to fulfill our purpose in Him, we must resolve
that today we will walk holy and righteous before Him, always
considering that what we do is done in His presence. We will
also therefore resolve to be innocent, **"without blame,"** not

doing anything to injure the name of the Lord or our fellow man. We do this by walking in love. These too are themes that are further elaborated on in this letter, and we will look at them in more depth later as well, but for now let's proceed with verse five which continues this amazing revelation of our purpose in Christ:

...having predestined us to adoption as sons by Jesus Christ to Himself, according to the good pleasure of His will (NKJV).

We were not only foreknown by the Lord, but we were predestined to be adopted by Him, to become His sons and daughters! Christians are the true royalty on the earth, and are honored by the heavenly host far above any earthly kings or presidents. This is His "good pleasure and His will." Nothing will ever be strong enough to thwart His will, and therefore our inheritance in Him is more secure than any earthly position ever could be.

Of course, none of us deserve such an inheritance. This will forever be one of the great testimonies of the grace and love of God. Even when we were yet sinners, He bought us for a price— the most valuable commodity in the universe—the blood of the Son of God. Since we value a thing by what someone is willing to pay for it, God Himself set a value on *you* that is more precious than anything else in creation—His own Son. If this is the value that God placed on us, how much more should we treasure our own lives, and the lives of one another, as the infinite treasures that they are, and not waste a single day frivolously?

You were predestined. You have a destiny. Your destiny is of more value than all of the treasure on earth. Therefore, invest in your destiny in Christ. There is no investment on earth that will ever pay greater dividends. Because a basic spiritual principle is **"... where your treasure is, there your heart will be also" (Matthew 6:21)**, the more we invest in our heavenly calling, the more at home we will be there, and the more of His glory and power that prevails in heaven will be manifested in our lives.

C H A P T E R   F I V E

The Wonders of Our Inheritance

We continue our study of Ephesians with verses six and seven of chapter one:

> **to the praise of the glory of His grace, by which He has made us accepted in the Beloved.**
>
> **In Him we have redemption through His blood, the forgiveness of sins, according to the riches of His grace... (NKJV).**

This is the most basic of all Christian truths, but one of the most difficult for us to comprehend—*we are accepted by God in Christ!* The fruit of the Tree of Knowledge of Good and Evil causes us to think that we must do something to earn our acceptance. Almost all of life is a constant battle to measure up to someone else's expectations, a continual judging and scoring of our performance by which we are either rewarded or punished. For us to receive the ultimate reward, adoption into the family of the King, by nothing but faith in Christ and *what He accomplished* on the cross, challenges the foundations of our entire life paradigm.

To even begin to comprehend this great truth results in nothing less than a transformation so great that we are born again. This is truly **"the riches of His grace."** An entire lifetime of pondering this one fact would not be enough to exhaust the revelation of the love of God manifested in the cross. However, to not grasp our acceptance in God through the cross alone, and not from our own efforts, is to continue eating from the Tree of Knowledge and its poisonous fruit instead of the fruit of the Tree of Life.

By reiterating this great and basic truth here, that we are redeemed by the blood of Jesus, have the forgiveness of sins through Him, and that all we receive is **"according to the riches of His grace,"** Paul is fortifying the foundational truths in order that he can further illuminate the glorious calling that we have in a way that will not feed our pride, but rather continually thrust our attention upon the glory and grace of God. We cannot walk in our inheritance if we are overly focused on ourselves and on what we have attained. We grow in our purpose by keeping our attention on the One who has called us, and by His grace equipped us. This is further expounded in verses eight through ten:

...which He lavished upon us. In all wisdom and insight

He made known to us the mystery of His will, according to His kind intention which He purposed in Him

with a view to an administration suitable to the fulness of the times, that is the summing up of all things in Christ, things in the heavens and things upon the earth. In Him.

As it has often been said, if we do not stay focused on the ultimate purpose of God, we will be continually distracted by the lesser purposes. Many are distracted from the River of Life by all of the little tributaries that feed it. The ultimate purpose of God in our lives is Christlikeness. The purpose of every trial in our lives is to help us to be conformed to His image. If we would keep this in mind, it would help us to understand everything that is going on in our lives. It would also help keep us from being distracted by the many lesser purposes that are constantly trying to draw us away from the Tree of Life who is Christ Himself.

This should also be the governing purpose in every thing to which we give our time and efforts. The apostolic mandate was not to build ministries, or even churches, but to labor until Christ was formed in His people (see Galatians 4:19). If we ever let anything eclipse this basic devotion, we have been distracted from the path of life. As Paul wrote in II Corinthians 11:3: **"But I am afraid, lest as the serpent deceived Eve by his craftiness, your minds should be led astray from the simplicity and purity of devotion to Christ."**

Having again established the Source of our grace and calling, Paul keeps on driving home these basics while beginning to include the nature of this awesome calling that we have, which we see in verses eleven through fourteen of chapter one:

...also we have obtained an inheritance, having been predestined according to His purpose who works all things after the counsel of His will,

to the end that we who were the first to hope in Christ should be to the praise of His glory.

In Him, you also, after listening to the message of truth, the gospel of your salvation—having also believed, you were sealed in Him with the Holy Spirit of promise,

who is given as a pledge of our inheritance, with a view to the redemption of God's own possession, to the praise of His glory.

We have obtained an inheritance, and it is nothing less than the inheritance of Christ! We are called as His bride—to be joint heirs with Him! This too is incomprehensible at first, far too wonderful, especially as we consider the sin and rebellion against God that we were delivered from. That He would take each of us who are deserving of eternal punishment, death forever, and not only give us eternal life, but share with us His own inheritance, is a love that in all of eternity we could not fathom.

It is no wonder that He is forever called the Lamb in heaven. There is no greater revelation of the riches of His grace, His love, and His forgiveness, than what He has done for us through His own sacrifice. Even as we attain the greatest spiritual maturity, and walk in the highest calling, we will never be too mature to bow our knees before what He did for us at the cross. If anyone ever thinks that they have matured beyond having a continual wonderment at the cross, they have not matured, but have made a very basic departure from the path of life. As we clearly read, even at the end of the age to come, all of heaven still marvels at Him and calls Him "the Lamb."

His pledge to us of this great inheritance as His joint heirs, is giving us His Holy Spirit to live in us now. All of the treasures on the earth are not worth having in exchange for the Holy Spirit to abide in us for one moment! Gratefully, He has been given to us freely to abide in us. How awesome is our God! How unfathomable are His ways! Surely, man in his most outrageous imagination has not been able to invent a story that is as wonderful as the truth of the gospel of Jesus Christ. How can we fail to walk in wonder and awe continually? How can any who know this great truth fail to share it continually? We love because He first loved us, and we share the story of His love because there is no greater story that will ever be told.

This is the great treasure that we have been given, the inheritance that has no equal in all of creation—our inheritance is the Lord Himself. We are called to be members of His household, members of His own eternal family. Eternal life is wonderful beyond comprehension. All of the power and glory and wonders of heaven are far beyond our present comprehension—but none of them are equal to the fact that we will be joined with Him in His own eternal family.

C H A P T E R   S I X

Love Renowned

We continue our study of Ephesians and the purpose of the church with Chapter 1:15-17:

For this reason I too, having heard of the faith in the Lord Jesus which exists among you, and your love for all the saints,

do not cease giving thanks for you, while making mention of you in my prayers;

that the God of our Lord Jesus Christ, the Father of glory, may give to you a spirit of wisdom and of revelation in the knowledge of Him.

Faith and love are the two great pillars of Christian character. These had begun to grow in the Ephesian church to the point that it was being talked about abroad. Could this be said of your church? Could this be said of you? First, are we even doing anything noteworthy enough to be talked about? If so, would it be said that faith and love exists among us?

I once had a visitation from the Lord in which He said only one thing to me, "You are now known all over the earth for many things, but none of them are love." Needless to say I was convicted. As Peter Lord used to say, "The main thing is to keep the main thing the main thing." I Timothy 1:5 states, **"But the goal of our instruction is love from a pure heart and a good**

conscience and a sincere faith." If the Lord's disciples are to be known by their love, I was guilty of missing the main thing.

How the church would be transformed if the entire body of Christ resolved to keep this main goal as growing in faith and love! What would happen if our reports were mostly of acts of faith and deeds of love? We probably would not be so concerned with how many people were coming to our meetings because we would always have too many.

It was because of the news of the Ephesians' faith and love that Paul was continually giving thanks for them in his prayers. This is truly the greatest joy that a spiritual father could ever have in his spiritual children.

It was also because of their increase in the truly important matters that Paul prayed for them to receive the spirit of wisdom and revelation of the Lord. When wisdom and revelation of the Lord begins to flow in a church, it is certainly destined for greatness, just as the Ephesian church was to become one of the truly extraordinary churches of the first century. However, our true greatness in the eternal chronicles of heaven will always be directly related to our faith and love, which is what true wisdom and true revelation must be built upon.

A worthy goal is the desire for our church to become so extraordinary that news of it is spread abroad. However, let us also be sure that we become known for the right reasons. It can all begin with you. Why not determine that your church is going to become famous for its faith and love? If just one person begins to grow in these it will be infectious. In what area of your life is the Lord dealing with you to grow in faith? Determine that you are going to believe and not doubt. Who are the most difficult people in your life to love? They are there for a reason. Do not waste your trials. These opportunities to grow are worth more than any earthly treasure. Invest where it will pay the greatest dividends, and pay them for eternity.

CHAPTER SEVEN

Eyes That See

In this chapter we will examine Ephesians 1:18:

I pray that the eyes of your heart may be enlightened, so that you may know what is the hope of His calling, what are the riches of the glory of His inheritance in the saints,

Did you ever consider that your heart has eyes? Have the eyes of your heart been opened yet? If we walk in the faith that we are called to, what we see with the eyes of our hearts will be more real to us than what we see with our natural eyes. The eyes of the heart are the eyes of the Spirit that can enable us to see further and more clearly than any natural eyes ever could.

Paul prayed for the opening of the spiritual eyes of the Ephesians so that they could know what is the hope of the Lord's calling not theirs, and what were **"the riches of the glory of His inheritance in the saints,"** not just what was the glory of their inheritance.

Many years ago the Lord spoke to me and said that a great deception had gone out over many of His people. This deception was the overemphasis on who we are in Christ in place of who He is in us. A key word to understanding this deception is "overemphasis." We do need to know who we are called to be in Christ, but true faith is not built up by seeing who we are, but by seeing who He is. True vision is seeing Him, who He is, and where He now sits. We will never be changed into His glory by seeing who we are, but by seeing Him.

Without question there is a high calling in Christ. When Paul was writing the book of Philippians near the end of his life, he stated that he did not think he had yet attained. He obviously was not talking about salvation, as he was saved on the day that he believed. What he was talking about was **"the high calling" (Philippians 3:14).** The Scriptures are clear that there are levels of rewards and levels of authority that will be given in heaven. These are determined by our obedience and faith in this life. Some will be given one city, some five, some ten, etc. There are some appointed who will sit on His right hand and on his left.

We see in Revelation 7 the great company that stands before the throne, but the overcomers in the Laodicean church are promised to sit with Him *on* His throne. I have talked to many Christian leaders who told me that they thought that not understanding this was the source for some of the greatest weaknesses in the Western church today. What we do here will count for eternity! However, the way we attain this high calling is not by seeking our own rewards, but rather by becoming devoted to seeing the Lord receive the reward of His inheritance.

If Paul the apostle could not know in this life what he had attained to in relation to **"the high calling,"** I think it is questionable that any of us could. If Paul did not think that he had yet attained, where does that leave us? It leaves us where it left him—pressing on! It is abundantly clear in Scripture that enduring to the end is crucial. Runners in track meets are trained to run through the finish line to a mark beyond it, so they will not slow down at the end. Not running through the finish line can actually cause us to stumble. How many great men and women of God have stumbled near the end of their lives?

The mark that we have been given to run to through our finish line is nothing less than Christlikeness. We are called to be like Him and do the works that He did. Who on the earth has yet attained to that? Those I have met who claimed to be the "sons of God" have appeared as some of the most foolish of all, like little children who put on Superman costumes and began thinking they were Superman. Just having a revelation of **"the high calling"** does not mean you have attained to it. Every Christian should have this revelation as it is clear in the Scriptures, but many have not yet had the "eyes of their heart opened" so as to see it.

When I inquired of the Lord many years ago about how we could know on this earth if we had attained to this **"high calling,"** He assured me that we could not know on this earth. He said that to attain it we had to be so consumed with seeing Jesus glorified that we would not even care about what we had personally attained. That is why the opening of the eyes of our hearts has to do with seeing His glory, and His inheritance, not our own.

The way for us to attain the great inheritance is not to be that concerned about it, but to be completely devoted to seeing our Lord receive the reward of His sacrifice. When we look at what He did for us, leaving all of the glory to come to earth, and live such an impoverished life as a man, and then to be so cruelly executed by the very ones He came to save, what could any of us ever do in comparison?

It is important to acknowledge that there is a **"high calling."** However, those who are overly focused on it have lost their way, have lost true vision, and will stumble over the things that could disqualify them from this **"high calling."** We can only attain by seeing Him, not ourselves. Let us pray with Paul that the eyes of our hearts will be opened to see Him, His calling, and His inheritance. Only then will we see everything else clearly.

CHAPTER EIGHT

Cultivating Power

In Ephesians 1:18, Paul wrote, **"I pray that the eyes of your heart may be enlightened, so that you may know what is the hope of His calling, what are the riches of the glory of His inheritance in the saints."** Then he continues in verse 19:

> **and what is the surpassing greatness of His power toward us who believe. These are in accordance with the working of the strength of His might.**

This is another one of those verses that is worthy of far more study than we can give it here. In fact, I wrote an entire book from it entitled, ***The Surpassing Greatness of His Power***. This is a crucial, pivotal understanding if we are going to walk in our full purpose. How can we be witnesses and representatives of the Almighty without power?

Paul stated the power that is offered to us is no less than the "working of the strength of the Lord's might!" The **"surpassing greatness of His power,"** the One who created all things, is extended to us who believe! Could this be possible? The Lord Jesus Himself stated in Matthew 17:20:

> **"...for truly I say to you, if you have faith as a mustard seed, you shall say to this mountain, 'Move from here to there,' and it shall move; and nothing shall be impossible to you."**

A mustard seed is not very big. In fact, it is very small. Certainly it would seem that every Christian has that much faith. All Christians have deposited within them faith that can do the most extraordinary exploits. Why do we not see this being exhibited?

In truth we have, to a degree. Christians are responsible for the greatest exploits in history. They have moved many mountains, and many more are about to be moved. Slavery was one of them. Feudalism was another, and the list goes on and on. Even so, the Lord was speaking of faith being able to move literal mountains, which we have not seen yet. We will. However, to do this we must have faith like a seed. A seed is something that we must cultivate, nurture, and protect, until it is mature and bears fruit.

If every Christian was immediately given authority to move mountains, the world would certainly be in chaos. The Lord has so instituted the laws of faith as to also require maturity, wisdom, and most important of all, obedience to the King. True faith is not a faith in our faith—it is faith in Jesus. Because it is faith in Him, it requires that we look to Him and see Him to believe. As we look to the King and see who He is, our faith will grow, and we will also bend our wills to His as we behold His great authority and glory.

True faith is obedience. This is why Paul wrote in Romans 1:5, **"through whom we have received apostleship to bring about *the obedience of faith* among all the Gentiles, for His name's sake."** If even Jesus did not do anything unless He saw the Father do it, how much more should we be under submission to do nothing that He does not show us to do? We may ask, "Can anyone live this way?" Yes. In fact we were created for it, and to walk any other way is contrary to our true nature.

Man was created to have fellowship with God, and to walk with Him daily just as Adam did before the Fall. Because of this there is a void in our soul that can only be filled by a daily encounter with the Lord. The new creation man is created for something even greater—we are created to actually be the dwelling place of God. He lives in us! The One who created the universe lives in each one of us. As Paul wrote in I Corinthians

3:16: "Do you not know that you are God's temple, and that God's Spirit dwells in you?" If anyone begins to really live by this truth, they will be able to easily move mountains and drop them into the sea.

Remember in the previous verse we studied, Ephesians 1:18, Paul prayed for "the eyes of our heart" to be opened. That is the key to miraculous power—seeing what the Lord is doing and becoming one with Him in it.

This does not happen for anyone all at once, as it did not even happen to Paul the apostle that way. He grew in the faith. Again, faith is like a seed that must be planted, cultivated, watered, nurtured until it bears fruit, and protected from weeds that would choke it. That is why Adam was given the job of cultivating the garden. Walking with God and cultivating what He has planted, is a fundamental purpose that we have on this earth. Are you cultivating the seeds that have been planted in your own heart? There is a seed in you that can move mountains. Start cultivating it right now by moving the obstacles that are in your life which are hindering your spiritual walk. Do not be satisfied with a faith less than that which can move a literal mountain. Someone is going to do this. Why not you?

C H A P T E R   N I N E

Ultimate Authority

In the last chapter we briefly addressed Ephesians 1:19, **"...the surpassing greatness of His power toward us who believe. These are in accordance with the working of the strength of His might."** It should be the ultimate goal of every Christian to live by the **"strength of His might"** and not just our own strength. The next four verses direct us to the way in which we do this:

> **which He brought about in Christ, when He raised Him from the dead, and seated Him at His right hand in the heavenly places,**
>
> **far above all rule and authority and power and dominion, and every name that is named, not only in this age, but also in the one to come.**
>
> **And He put all things in subjection under His feet, and gave Him as head over all things to the church,**
>
> **which is His body, the fulness of Him who fills all in all.**

True faith is not an emotion or feeling. It is not even just confidence that something can be done. True faith is the recognition of who Jesus is and the authority that He has. Miracles are done in His name. This means they are done by His authority, not our own. We will never be able to do great works of healing because we are a great apostle or prophet, because we have written great books, or because we have built a great church. All true spiritual authority comes from His throne, not our own position. Therefore, our goal should be to gain authority with Him, not just over people or things. How do we do this? Hebrews 11:6 tells us:

And without faith it is impossible to please Him, for he who comes to God must believe that He is, and that He is a rewarder of those who seek Him.

We do need to settle in our hearts that it requires faith to please God. Faith is not just believing that He can or will do great things, but it is trust—for the present! If we are going to come to God we must believe that He *is*. This is much more than just believing that He exists. Many claim to have faith in the Bible because they believe the things written in it literally happened, but that is not true faith in the Bible or in God. True faith is believing all of the things that were written in the Bible in order to see them happen in our own lives. True faith is for what *is*, not just what *was*.

As someone once said, "God is not an Author who wrote just one book and then retired!" He is still doing everything today that He did when the Scriptures were written. He is the same today as He was then. His name is not "I was," or "I will be," but it is "I Am!" True faith begins with seeing the depth of God's love that was forever demonstrated for us on the cross, and going beyond the cross to see Him in the power of His resurrection. True faith is seeing Jesus where He is today, above all rule, authority, and dominion.

The Lord wants to intervene in your personal life today. If we converted the time that we usually spend worrying about our problems into prayer, we would see more and more of His activity in our lives. By this our faith grows. Do not believe for one moment that He does not want to be bothered by our little problems. To turn to Him for help is in fact what pleases Him! As we see Him intervene in the little things, we will grow in faith for bigger things. Faith really is like a muscle. The more you use it, the bigger it grows. If you do not use it, atrophy will set in. The Lord wants you to exercise your faith, so do not miss a single opportunity to do it.

PART II

A Vision of a Heavenly Walk

A Study of Ephesians Chapter 2

CHAPTER TEN

Seated With Him Above

O ur study begins with Ephesians 2:1-4:

And you were dead in your trespasses and sins,

In which you formerly walked according to the course of this world, according to the prince of the power of the air, of the spirit that is now working in the sons of disobedience.

Among them we too all formerly lived in the lusts of our flesh, indulging in the desires of the flesh and the mind, and were by nature children of wrath, even as the rest.

But God, being rich in mercy, because of His great love with which He loved us.

We may consider ourselves to be good people, but even the best people on earth are still motivated by selfish interests until they are born again in Christ. Even if we are religious it will be for selfish gain, to appear as righteous to others, or for the good of man from an earthly perspective rather than a heavenly one. When we are still in our trespasses we may not be able to see such evil motives in ourselves, but when we are born again we can assert with Romans 3:10-12:

There is none righteous, not even one.

There is none who understands, there is none who seeks for God;

All have turned aside, together they have become useless; There is none who does good. There is not even one.

We affirm therefore that we are no better than anyone else—we have simply found mercy. It is the realization of the great mercy of God that causes us to marvel at His goodness, and for which we cannot help but love Him. It is by this love that the goodness in Him begins to grow in us. Even so, as the apostle Paul was so wise to convey in all of his writings, it is a good thing to continually be reminded of where we came from, and how great His mercy is toward us.

In our text for this chapter we also see that we walked according to the "prince of the air." Before Christ intervened in our lives, we all walked according to the ways of this world—the ways of "the prince of the air," which is Satan. Because he is not omnipresent, he does his work through other evil spirits that operate on a regional basis called principalities. This refers to them as the principle influence over a region.

The "prince of the air" over a region is generally identified by the primary evil attributes of the people in that region. However, there is some basic understanding about these principalities and powers that we must have if we are going to discern them correctly.

Just as no person has only one personality trait, princes over regions will usually have multiple characteristics. For example, in the region where I live there is a strong spirit of poverty over the mountain people. A spirit of poverty can cause people to be underachievers. It does this by making them think less of themselves and their talents than they should. Some of our neighbors are people of extraordinary talent and intelligence, but they think and often say, they are "just poor folks" or "nothing special." In fact, they are quite special. As we know, God gives His grace to the humble. But there is a difference between humility and an inferiority complex, which makes one an underachiever and keeps them underemployed. Even the Christians in the region tend to see themselves as "poor sinners," rather than overcomers in Christ. While this is not true of them all, because some do see the truth of the Scriptures that sets them free from these yokes, there is the prevailing spirit of poverty in our region of the mountains in North Carolina.

The spirit of poverty may be the foundational yoke of bondage, but it is combined by other factors such as a fierce territorial spirit that works alongside it. This territorial spirit causes people to feel intimidated by outsiders or people who are different. There is also a spirit of delusion in regions that feed addictive behaviors like alcoholism and drug use. All of this has set up many children in the region to be open to witchcraft and spiritualism because cults draw those with inferiority complexes. Have you ever heard of an usher or deacon in a satanic cult? No, because everyone is made to think that they are called to be a "high priest." This particular deception draws those who feel inferior by making them feel special.

Only an hour away in Charlotte, a very different spirit is prevailing over that city. In place of the inferiority that the people in the mountains feel, in the city there is much arrogance with people thinking more highly of themselves than they should. In Charlotte there is a spirit of charismatic witchcraft instead of the kind of spiritualism found in the mountains. This has nothing to do with the Charismatic Movement, but rather is a tendency to use human charisma to manipulate and control others.

Because MorningStar has churches in both locations we greatly adjust our messages and strategy for each place. We try to impart confidence and faith to the people in the mountains because there are some world-class artists, musicians, and potential leaders who have a hard time seeing their own gifts. We preach much more about humility in the city where many conflicts arise out of selfish ambition and pride. We have also started an interchange between the churches in both regions so that they can help each other.

It can be very helpful to understand how we walk according to the "prince of the air" over a region so as not to allow it to control or influence our lives. As a result, we can preach the truth that will set people free. It is by seeing how our nature was in conflict with the truth, and how desperately we need the grace of God that is given to us through the cross, that we are set free and can become true freedom fighters that help set others free. This is our purpose, as we see expounded in Ephesians 2:5-7:

> **even when we were dead in our transgressions, made us alive together with Christ (by grace you have been saved),**
>
> **and raised us up with Him and seated us with Him in the heavenly places, in Christ Jesus,**
>
> **in order that in the ages to come He might show the surpassing riches of His grace in kindness toward us in Christ Jesus.**

The way we counter the evil "prince of the air," is for us to be raised above him and seated with Christ. When we do this, and begin to see His glory and magnificence, it is much easier to discern and resist "the prince of the air."

For eternity, we will be uncovering layer after layer of the revelation of God's unfathomable ways, and His grace and love that is revealed through the cross. Even though we walked in all of the evil that required God Himself to suffer as He did because of our sin, He not only forgave and saved us, but He enabled us to sit with Him on His throne. This is so remarkable that very few people actually believe it enough to do it.

I have a friend who is a king in Ghana, West Africa. In one conversation he explained that when he is in his domain and sits on his throne, no one may approach him unless they are invited. The fact that the Lord has given us an open invitation to come boldly into His presence before His throne of grace was more than amazing to him. That the Lord would also allow us to sit with Him on His throne, which is nothing less than sharing His authority, was almost incomprehensible.

It would be one of the greatest privileges on earth to be able to walk into the Oval Office of the President at any time, but how much more wonderful that we can boldly come before the throne of the King of kings! However, we must go beyond believing this to actually doing it if we are going to fulfill our purpose on this earth.

To comprehend this great truth, we must cease trying to earn it. We will never, in ourselves, be worthy of the greatest of honors and responsibilities. This was attained for us by Jesus. It is not something that He is doing grudgingly, rather He wants us to sit with Him in His seat of authority so much so that He endured the shame and the pain of the cross for it. We may wonder, if the Lord wants us to have it so much, why does He not make it easier? Why does He require us to do this by faith, rather than just send an honor guard of angels to escort us to our seat with Him?

Satan fell because he wanted that seat so badly he tried to seize it by his own power. True faith is in Jesus, not in ourselves or our own faith. True faith is therefore growing in dependence on Jesus. As we grow in faith in Him and His accomplishments at the cross—not on how righteous we are becoming or what we have accomplished, He can then trust us with more power and authority because we will only exercise it in unity with Him. Our calling is not to sit on His throne, but to sit with Him on His throne.

Jesus did not do anything except what He saw the Father doing. He walked in union with His Father. We too must do the same with Him. We only have true spiritual authority to the degree that we are abiding in Him. The angels do not respect us and the demons do not obey us because of who we are, but because of Who is in us.

CHAPTER ELEVEN

The Gift of God

As we proceed to Ephesians 2:8-9, we observe how the apostle continues a most crucial understanding for believers who will walk in their purpose:

For by grace you have been saved through faith; and that not of yourselves, it is the gift of God;

not as a result of works, that no one should boast.

Why does Paul continue to review something so basic after explaining to the Ephesians that they were called to such lofty things as being seated with Christ in the heavenly places? He does this because in this life the tendency of trying to establish our place with the Lord on the basis of our own works will be a constant temptation. The more spiritual authority we are given, the greater this temptation can become. Paul tirelessly reminded the disciples that they were not saved by works but by faith in the finished work of Christ. He comprehended accurately that the greatest challenge to the truth of the gospel was for Satan to seduce believers into substituting works for the power of the cross in their lives.

Now, almost 2,000 years later, this is still a primary test that tempts every believer, every church, and every movement, causing many to stumble. This is actually the same test that Adam and Eve faced in the garden—would they live by the knowledge of good and evil, or by the fruit of the Tree of Life? We must understand that in this life we will be continually confronted with the same choice. If the "good" we see in ourselves outweighs the evil, we will feel better about ourselves and think that God should too. Isn't the whole point that He wants us to be good? However, that is a basic departure from the faith that leads to true goodness and deliverance from the evil that has gripped us. As Paul explained repeatedly in his letters, if believers tried to stand on the works of the Law for righteousness, they would be severed from Christ. It is that crucial a choice.

The Law revealed the standards of God's righteousness. It also revealed that no man could live by it, so sacrifices for sin were necessary. When Christ, the pure, spotless Lamb of God came and gave His own life to pay for our sin, He became our salvation. To reject Him and try to come on the basis of our own works is the ultimate pride, delusion, and insult to the grace of God that He provided for us. That will never change. We will never be able to stand before God because we have been good, but we can come boldly before His throne at any time by the blood of the Son of God. Jesus alone is our righteousness.

Those who begin to trust in their own works inevitably grow in pride in themselves, not in Christ. They will be the most offended by those who claim righteousness based on faith, such as the young Paul, "the Pharisee of Pharisees," who was offended by the young church. It was this that drove him to persecute the church and brought him into direct conflict with the truth. It was this result of his own self-righteousness that probably enabled him to grasp the nature of this conflict with a greater depth than most of the others of his time.

The conflict that drove Paul to persecute the young church had its roots in the original conflict between brothers that caused Cain to slay his brother Abel. Cain's offering was rejected because he offered the fruit of his own labors, while Abel offered a blood sacrifice that prophesied of the coming of Christ. This led to a rage in Cain that caused him to slay his brother. The cross is the basis of our acceptance to God and remains the primary point of conflict between Christianity and every other religion, which are all based on man's acceptance through works.

If we are truly following Christ, and He is our righteousness, our boast will always be in Him. How could we ever think highly of our own works when we have beheld what He has done? For us to even presume that anything we could do would make us acceptable is an affront to the cross and the ultimate form of pride that will lead to a fall, ultimately severing us from Christ.

It is by beholding His great love for us, which He proved by suffering as He did on our behalf, that we are compelled to love and follow Him. It is as we walk in the knowledge of the salvation for which He endured so much on our behalf that we gain increasing freedom, and boldness as we trust Him, not ourselves.

As Jesus explained, the Father loves us too. In fact, it was the Father who loved us so much that He sent His beloved Son to die for us. The Father loves us that much, but He will never accept us by our own works. For Him to do so is to nullify the cross, and to leave us in the grip of the pride that caused sin and death in the first place.

Now we proceed with the next verse in our study, Ephesians 2:10:

For we are His workmanship, created in Christ Jesus for good works, which God prepared beforehand, that we should walk in them.

In this way Paul brilliantly launches out from the understanding that we are not saved by works in order to fortify the truth that we are the Lord's workmanship, and not our own. In the world "self-made" men and women are esteemed, but not so in Christ. Our goal is to be fashioned and established by the grace of God, not our own efforts. In this way we are **"His workmanship,"** devoted to becoming what He wants us to be.

After declaring that we are not saved by works, Paul then states that we are nevertheless created for **"good works."** There is a difference between doing good works in order to gain acceptance and doing good works from the position of having God's acceptance. We are not working in order to gain approval, but because we love the One who loved us, saved us, and works through us.

When we begin to comprehend that we are Christ's workmanship, that He is actually using everything in our lives, we understand that nothing happens in our lives that is not allowed by God for our perfecting. He is the Potter, and we are the clay. We are spinning on the Potter's wheel of life and the events of our life are His hands shaping us. Our goal should be to become easy for Him to work with by not resisting His dealings in our lives, and by allowing ourselves to be shaped by them.

This is seldom easy and sometimes can be quite confusing. We want to submit to God, but we are called to resist the devil. Some of the events in our lives are from the devil, so how do we distinguish between them? Also, some of the dealings of God in our lives that will mature us include letting the devil test us. Do we submit to these too?

It might be easier if there were very simple answers to these questions, but if there were, we would not have to seek the Lord and His wisdom. There are answers to situations that can indeed be quite complex, requiring wisdom from above to understand. Even so, the way through every situation and trial is to follow Christ. As we are told in II Corinthians 2:14: **"But thanks be to God, who always leads us in His triumph in Christ, and manifests through us the sweet aroma of the knowledge of Him in every place."** He **"leads us in His triumph,"** which means that we must follow Him. That is always the right answer— to follow Him.

For this we must seek Him, see Him, and keep our attention on Him. This is the purpose of almost every trial in our lives, and the finished work of every trial is for us to be closer to Him. The quicker we give ourselves to finding Him, and the more resolute we are in following Him through a trial, the quicker we will usually emerge from it.

However, following Him always leads to the cross. His triumph was the cross, and it is ours too. That is why He said in Matthew 16:25, **"For whoever wishes to save his life shall lose it; but whoever loses his life for My sake shall find it."** If we are in Christ we are to be dead to this world. It is impossible to offend a dead person. It is impossible for a dead person to feel rejected or abused. If this is true we can respond to any situation with God's love. In this way through our triumph over every trial He **"manifests through us the sweet aroma of the knowledge of Him in every place."**

To simplify our situation we might ask: "Is my response to this trial manifesting Christ? If not, how do I need to change my response to this situation to manifest Him?" The simple: "What Would Jesus Do?" is our answer. As we do this we will be conformed to His image, becoming His workmanship which is being manifested to this world.

As this verse also states, we were created in Him **"for good works."** This is a primary theme in the book of James. As we read in James 2:18-24:

> **But someone may well say, "You have faith, and I have works; show me your faith without the works, and I will show you my faith by my works."**
>
> **You believe that God is one. You do well; the demons also believe, and shudder.**
>
> **But are you willing to recognize, you foolish fellow, that faith without works is useless?**
>
> **Was not Abraham our father justified by works, when he offered up Isaac his son on the altar?**
>
> **You see that faith was working with his works, and as a result of the works, faith was perfected;**
>
> **and the Scripture was fulfilled which says, "And Abraham believed God, and it was reckoned to him as righteousness," and he was called the friend of God.**
>
> **You see that a man is justified by works, and not by faith alone.**

James was protesting the very delusion that multitudes of Christians today fall prey to—just believing in the Lord's existence is enough to be "saved." As James explained, the demons believe in the Lord, knowing His power and authority probably much more than most Christians. If we really believe the Lord, we will live for Him, obey Him, and do the works that He created us for.

CHAPTER TWELVE

From Death to Life

In the next verse, Ephesians 2:11, Paul continues his teaching on how we are transformed and prepared for our purpose in Christ:

> **Therefore remember, that formerly you, the Gentiles in the flesh, who are called "Uncircumcision" by the so-called "Circumcision," which is performed in the flesh by human hands ...**

Why would the Lord make circumcision a sign of His covenant with man? The **"flesh"** is often a metaphor for the carnal nature in Scripture, which was to be a sign for us that to be joined to the Lord in covenant, the carnal nature had to be cut away.

Circumcision was instituted in the beginning of His process to redeem man from the Fall, when He called Abraham. What it represents continues to be a requirement for all who would be reconciled to the Lord. Salvation is much more than just having our sins forgiven. The salvation of the cross also provides for the removal of our sinful nature, **"the body of sin" (Romans 6:6).**

It is a delusion and a tragic perversion of the gospel that promotes an easy forgiveness without the corresponding laying aside of the sinful nature. As we read repeatedly throughout the New Testament, and see clearly established in the Old Testament, those who have truly embraced the atonement of the cross have also been born again and changed by it.

Now let us consider something about circumcision and how it relates to the removal of our sinful nature. I do not mean to be indelicate, but we should note that the whole member was not cut off. Only the excessive flesh (which represents the sinful nature) is removed by circumcision. Our whole nature is not sinful. The Lord created us flesh and blood with certain needs and desires that He intends for us to fulfill with joy and thanksgiving. Having these desires is not sin.

When the term **"flesh"** is used in Scripture it is in relationship to the sinful nature, not that which is natural. The desire for sex, for example, is not sin when it is kept within the boundaries for which it was created. It is a special gift from God to be enjoyed and used for the bonding of two people in the covenant relationship of marriage and is intended to be wonderful and exciting. This is important to understand because the best defense against having our natural desires perverted is to use them properly.

When I lived in Charlotte I often attended a weekly fellowship of pastors and leaders. I really enjoyed this fellowship because it seemed that something interesting happened every week. Though I was not present when this particular event took place, I was told about how a retired Anglican bishop, who must have been near eighty years old, once asked the other pastors to pray for him because of the sin in his life. When asked what it was he replied shamefully, "lust." Then he meekly added... "for my wife." At first everyone looked at him with disbelief, but when they saw he was serious, the other pastors responded in unison, "No, we don't need to pray for you. You need to pray for us!"

The whole purpose of redemption is to recover what was lost by the Fall—foremost was man's intimate relationship with God. Only when that is recovered can the relationship between people be restored to what it was intended to be. In all relationships, selfishness perverts. Therefore, we must be healed of the wounds of sin that cause selfishness such as rejection, abuse, etc. However, the way the Lord does this is not by a long process of introspection and digging around in our souls to find them—He cuts away the problems by having us start all over as born again new creations. The goal of having our minds renewed is so we can embrace the new creation that we now are, not try to fix the old man that is reckoned as dead.

We have another clear articulation of how this is wrought in our lives in Romans 6:3-14:

> Or do you not know that all of us who have been baptized into Christ Jesus have been baptized into His death?
>
> Therefore we have been buried with Him through baptism into death, so that as Christ was raised from the dead through the glory of the Father, so we too might walk in newness of life.
>
> For if we have become united with Him in the likeness of His death, certainly we shall also be in the likeness of His resurrection,
>
> knowing this, that our old self was crucified with Him, in order that our body of sin might be done away with, so that we would no longer be slaves to sin;
>
> for he who has died is freed from sin.
>
> Now if we have died with Christ, we believe that we shall also live with Him,
>
> knowing that Christ, having been raised from the dead, is never to die again; death no longer is master over Him.
>
> For the death that He died, He died to sin, once for all; but the life that He lives, He lives to God.
>
> Even so consider yourselves to be dead to sin, but alive to God in Christ Jesus.
>
> Therefore do not let sin reign in your mortal body so that you obey its lusts,
>
> and do not go on presenting the members of your body to sin as instruments of unrighteousness; but present yourselves to God as those alive from the dead, and your members as instruments of righteousness to God.
>
> For sin shall not be master over you...

CHAPTER THIRTEEN

The New Man

In the next verses in our study, Ephesians 2:12-16, the apostle explains another basic, but truly remarkable result of the cross and its work:

> **remember that you were at that time separate from Christ, excluded from the commonwealth of Israel, and strangers to the covenants of promise, having no hope and without God in the world.**

> **But now in Christ Jesus you who formerly were far off have been brought near by the blood of Christ.**

> **For He Himself is our peace, who made both groups into one and broke down the barrier of the dividing wall,**

> **by abolishing in His flesh the enmity, which is the Law of commandments contained in ordinances, so that in Himself He might make the two into one new man, thus establishing peace,**

> **and might reconcile them both in one body to God through the cross, by it having put to death the enmity.**

The Jews and the Gentiles are the **"two"** that Paul is talking about making into **"one new man."** One of the critical issues of our time is the revelation of how this is going to happen, and why. Many are beginning to understand that the modern church's foundation is based more in Rome than in Jerusalem. For many this is not a bad thing, but it is not what God intended. This is not to say that He did not want Rome, or the other great churches of the Gentiles to build upon the foundation—He just did not want them to supplant the chosen foundation for their own.

There is a reason why the Lord chose the Jewish people to bring forth Christ. There is also a reason why He laid the foundation of His church in Jerusalem, and why all of the writers of the Bible were Jewish. Understanding His reasons for this will be critical for entering into the full purpose of God before the end of this age. Even so, there is a ditch on both sides of the path of life, and very few have been able to find the path of life on this issue without falling into either side of it.

When many begin to comprehend the importance of understanding the Jewish roots, they swing back too far, and try to return to the "Law that is contained in ordinances" as a basis for their standing with God. As these verses in Ephesians declare, Jesus abolished this in His own flesh. He abolished it as a source of righteousness by becoming our righteousness at the cross. We therefore no longer seek to keep the Law for righteousness, but we embrace the cross and seek to abide in the Lord who is our righteousness. To really understand the true Jewish roots we actually have to go back before the Law, which was added because of transgressions. As we are most gravely warned in Galatians 5:4-9:

> **You have been severed from Christ, you who are seeking to be justified by law; you have fallen from grace.**
>
> **For we through the Spirit, by faith, are waiting for the hope of righteousness.**
>
> **For in Christ Jesus neither circumcision nor uncircumcision means anything, but faith working through love.**
>
> **You were running well; who hindered you from obeying the truth?**
>
> **This persuasion did not come from Him who calls you.**
>
> **A little leaven leavens the whole lump of dough.**

As we are warned, if we turn to the Law itself we are in danger of being **"severed from Christ."** I have watched many who began to understand the need to recover the Jewish roots of the church, and embrace the very leaven that Jesus warned about when He said in Matthew 16:6, **"...Watch out and beware of the leaven of the Pharisees and Sadducees."** This leaven is why we are also told that the Law is **"the ministry of death,"** and the **"ministry of condemnation" (II Corinthians 3:7,9).** However, as the same writer, Paul, also asserted in Romans 3:31, **"Do we then nullify the Law through faith? May it never be! On the contrary, we establish the Law."**

Neither did Jesus come to abolish the Law as the standard of God's righteousness. He came to fulfill it so that He could become our righteousness. As Paul also explained to the Romans, without the Law there would have been no transgression because there would have been no understanding of God's standards of righteousness. In this way the Law was our schoolteacher which led us to Christ. It led us to Him because of one certainty that every true seeker of God will come to realize—we cannot keep the Law by our own strength, which casts us completely upon the atonement of the cross for our forgiveness and reconciliation to God. This is explained in Romans 7:7-13:

> **What shall we say then? Is the Law sin? May it never be! On the contrary, I would not have come to know sin except through the Law; for I would not have known about coveting if the Law had not said, "You shall not covet."**
>
> **But sin, taking opportunity through the commandment, produced in me coveting of every kind; for apart from the Law sin is dead.**
>
> **And I was once alive apart from the Law; but when the commandment came, sin became alive, and I died;**
>
> **and this commandment, which was to result in life, proved to result in death for me;**
>
> **for sin, taking opportunity through the commandment, deceived me, and through it killed me.**

So then, the Law is holy, and the commandment is holy and righteous and good.

Therefore did that which is good become a cause of death for me? May it never be! Rather it was sin, in order that it might be shown to be sin by effecting my death through that which is good, that through the commandment sin might become utterly sinful.

One serious problem that we have in the church is a lack of the proper use of the Law, which is to reveal sin. This is often the tragic result of the gospel having been changed from Jesus having come to deliver us from sin to Him coming to deliver us from troubles. We will not cast ourselves upon the cross for forgiveness of our sins—the only basis for our reconciliation to God, if we do not realize that we are transgressors who need forgiveness and reconciliation. However, even though the Law is given to reveal sin, it is a deadly trap to embrace it as the remedy for sin in place of the cross.

So the Law is good if used as it was intended and is an ultimate deception and a **"ministry of death"** if used wrongly. Some use it rightly, and are compelled by it to go to the cross for reconciliation to God, but then return to the Law to try to keep its ordinances as a basis for continuing in God's approval, which is exactly the trap that Paul repeatedly addressed in his Epistles. This is the original heresy that the first century apostles had to fight, and one that is rising up again at the end. Ultimately, this is the choice between the Tree of the Knowledge of Good and Evil versus the Tree of Life.

As we read in our verses for this chapter, only the cross can abolish the enmity between Jew and Gentile, and bring the two together into one new man as will happen before the end. This will bring forth a tree with Jewish roots and Gentile branches, both of which need each other to survive and bear fruit. Jewish believers in Messiah will never be made complete without Gentile believers, and vice versa. Before the end comes, this will happen, but at the present time neither side has crawled out of their ditch to be joined on the road that is between them, the path of life.

CHAPTER FOURTEEN

The Test

And He came and preached peace to you who were far away, and peace to those who were near;

for through Him we both have our access in one Spirit to the Father.

So then you are no longer strangers and aliens, but you are fellow citizens with the saints, and are of God's household (Ephesians 2: 17-19).

The gospel that led us to salvation was a message of peace. In II Corinthians 13:5 we are exhorted to, **"Test yourselves to see if you are in the faith; examine yourselves!"** One of the primary tests of whether we are continuing on the path of life is by the peace in our lives. Jesus is the Prince of Peace, and if we are walking close to Him there will be a peace in our lives that exceeds anything that can be known in this world without Him.

If there is a lack of peace in our lives, if there is striving and anxiety, then we have drifted from Him. If this is the case, we certainly need to heed the exhortation to "examine ourselves!" Where did we miss the turn? What has come into our lives that began to eclipse our relationship with Him?

We are told that through Jesus we **"have our access in one Spirit to the Father."** The basic purpose of the atonement is to restore the relationship between God and man. Is this being accomplished in our lives? The primary way we can determine the degree to which redemption has worked in our lives is by how close we are to the Lord. This is a fundamental way that we can test the degree to which we are still walking in truth. Are we getting ever closer to the Lord?

This also relates to the next verse, we are **"no longer strangers and aliens, but are fellow citizens with the saints, and are of God's household."** One way I can tell how close I am to someone is by how comfortable I feel in their house. There are some people that I feel so comfortable with that I do not even have to ask if I can go to their refrigerator and get something to eat or drink. If I was in the home of someone I did not know very well, I would never presume to do something like that. However, I am never going to be as comfortable in anyone else's house as I am in my own. How comfortable do you feel in God's house? I am not talking about a church building, but rather in His presence, in the midst of His people.

The Lord's household is our house too. We are not strangers, and should never feel like strangers in His house. This does take time for any new believer, but it is another way by which we can measure how we are doing. Where do we feel the most at home? This is what is elaborated in II Corinthians 5:6-8:

> **Therefore, being always of good courage, and knowing that while we are at home in the body we are absent from the Lord—**
>
> **for we walk by faith, not by sight—**
>
> **we are of good courage, I say, and prefer rather to be absent from the body and to be at home with the Lord.**

Do we feel more comfortable walking by faith than by what we see? Are we becoming more at home in the heavenly realm than in the natural? As Joe Garlington once said, "We are not human beings having a temporary spiritual experience, but we are spiritual beings having a temporary human experience."

One of the popular hip questions today is "Who's your daddy?" When you think of your father, who do you think of first? Is it your Father in heaven or your earthly father? We might also ask, "Where is your home?" When you think of home, where to do you think of first?

CHAPTER FIFTEEN

The Foundation and the Capstone

For this chapter we will begin with Ephesians 2:20:

Having been built upon the foundation of the apostles and prophets, Christ Jesus Himself being the cornerstone.

Paul is not saying that the apostles and prophets are the foundation. As he wrote in I Corinthians 3:11, Jesus Christ is the only foundation for the church. It is the apostles and prophets who lay the foundation, which is Jesus. Jesus is not only the Cornerstone and the Foundation—He is the whole building.

In biblical times, engineers did not have elaborate plans drawn on large sheets of paper to work from. Instead they used the cornerstone of a building, which was made to be a scale of the building's shape and dimensions. That is why the cornerstone of the pyramids was also the capstone. During construction they would continually refer back to the cornerstone to be sure that they were complying with the architect's plan.

In this same way, Jesus is our Cornerstone. He is what is being built. This is what Paul summed up as the purpose of his work, and is the essence of true apostolic and prophetic ministry, as we read in Colossians 1:28-29:

and we proclaim Him, admonishing every man and teaching every man with all wisdom, that we may present every man complete in Christ.

And for this purpose also I labor, striving according to His power, which mightily works within me.

Paul was not just trying to get people to confess Jesus as their Savior, though that is certainly an important beginning. He was not just trying to get them to understand Christian doctrine accurately, though that too is important. This was also about much more than just planting churches wherever he went. All of these were but a means to the end—having each believer, conformed to the image of Christ. This is the image of God that many were originally created to bear. This begins with reconciliation to God through the atonement of the cross. After the atonement, comes the renewing of our minds and the conforming of our lives to His ways.

Again, God does not judge the condition or quality of His church by how good the meetings are on Sunday morning, but by how good the people are on Monday morning. The main calling of our lives is more than just knowing the truth—it is having that truth become our life.

The main purpose of the church is more than just providing ministry to the people—it is laboring until each one is conformed to the image of Christ. That is the foundation of apostolic and prophetic ministry, and what they are called to impart to all of the ministries in the church. This is the foundation of ministry—laboring for each one to be made **"complete in Christ."**

How does our ministry measure up when judged on this basis? The quality of our ministry is determined by the quality of the people we minister to in their daily lives. How are they at home? How are they when at work? How patient, loving, and kind are they when shopping or in traffic? How do they live in secret when no one else is around to see them? Are they becoming more like Christ? This should be how we judge our own lives. Are we more like Christ this year than last year? Is that the fruit of our ministry in the people's lives that we minister to?

Church history is similar to the history of Israel in Scripture. It is a continuous cycle of revival and deliverance followed by apathy, apostasy, bondage, and then the revival and deliverance that starts the cycle over again. The apathy usually turned into apostasy when rituals were used to replace the truths that they represented, or in more modern times, projects are used as a substitute for the life of Christ in our midst. There is nothing wrong with rituals when they are used properly, or with projects when they are kept in their place of secondary importance. However, we can possibly point to every major problem the church has had in history, and possibly in our own individual lives, as a result of being distracted from our primary purpose— being conformed to the image of Christ. Likewise, all ministry that is not primarily devoted to the conforming of others to the image of Christ has been distracted.

After addressing the crucial issue of getting the foundation right, the apostle then begins his discourse on how the construction of the temple of the Lord is to be completed with verses 21-22:

> **In whom the whole building, being fitted together is growing into a holy temple in the Lord;**
>
> **in whom you also are being built together into a dwelling of God in the Spirit.**

By this Scripture we can understand that we do not automatically become the temple of the Lord, rather it is something we grow into. How do we do this? We must be built together with other believers. One of the sure ways we can determine that we are being built into the temple of the Lord is by how our lives are being intermeshed with those of other believers. Church is not meant to be just a pile of living stones, but living stones that are fit together and cemented into their right places. Is this taking place in the congregation we are in? If not, why?

Church is not just a meeting—it is a life. Once we are born again and become a part of the new creation, our identity with the new creation should be much stronger than any natural ties that we have. Natural families tend to grow further apart, though they may gather regularly to keep their identity and relationships. However, the family of God does not just gather on holidays and special occasions to keep our relationships going—we gather continually. We gather to grow closer together, and our lives should be increasingly bonded together if we are growing into the temple we are called to be.

We must have a vision for our gatherings to be a time when the relationships within our congregations are built and strengthened. This is much more than just having people stand up for two minutes to greet each other. This is more than just having picnics and church socials, though these can be helpful. The temple of the Lord is called to be something more substantial than any other human relationship on earth.

How can our gatherings promote the building together of believers rather than just being meetings where the shepherds throw some food to the sheep? There are many practical ways we can do this. However, before we really understand the practical steps that are needed, we must receive the vision and heart for it. True church life is supposed to be an actual culture that is so wonderful, compelling, genuine, and real, that any who behold it are caused to marvel and wonder at it. When we have a true taste of this, we will not be able to get to the gatherings of God's people often enough.

Every gathering is supposed to be an experience where we leave edified and are built together with others so we grow closer to them as well. Before the end of this age, there will be a true church life as it was intended to be demonstrated on the earth. It will be a society within a society that is the richest and deepest of all human relationships on earth.

Even so, and even better than that will be the fact that we will be a temple for the Lord, and He will dwell among us. There is nothing that bonds people together stronger than experiencing the manifest presence of the Lord together. The Lord Himself is the true cement that holds His temple together. Even more important than getting closer to one another is getting closer to Him. If we are truly getting closer to the Lord, we will be getting closer to one another as well.

PART III

An Expanding Vision

A Study of Ephesians Chapter 3

CHAPTER SIXTEEN

An Inclusive Vision

W e now begin an important part of our journey through the book of Ephesians. In the first two chapters the apostle Paul gave the framework of a glorious and expansive vision of what Christians are called to be. For the remaining chapters of the Epistle, he lays out a practical plan for how this is achieved. We now continue our study with Ephesians 3:1-6:

> **For this reason I, Paul, the prisoner of Christ Jesus for the sake of you Gentiles—**
>
> **if indeed you have heard of the stewardship of God's grace which was given to me for you;**
>
> **that by revelation there was made known to me the mystery, as I wrote before in brief.**
>
> **And by referring to this, when you read you can understand my insight into the mystery of Christ,**
>
> **which in other generations was not made known to the sons of men, as it has now been revealed to His holy apostles and prophets in the Spirit;**
>
> **to be specific, that the Gentiles are fellow heirs and fellow members of the body, and fellow partakers of the promise in Christ Jesus through the gospel.**

Many think that the understanding of this "mystery" is elementary. However, it appears evident that very few Christians throughout church history, or today, really understand this "mystery" of how the Gentiles are grafted into the body of Christ, and have become fellow partakers of the promises of God. It is obvious that if the church understood this it would be very different than it is today. However, this "mystery" will be revealed, and when it is, we can expect some very radical changes in the way the church is manifested in the world.

When the Lord began the implementation of His redemptive plan by calling Abraham, He explained that Abraham's seed would be like the sand of the seashore and the stars of heaven. This indicated both a heavenly and earthly seed. The lack of understanding in this area is the reason there continues to be confusion about the place of both Israel and the church for God's plans in the last days. Some believe the church has supplanted Israel in all of the promises, and others believe Israel will supplant the church at the end. Neither of these are accurate. From the beginning God intended that there would be both a spiritual and a natural seed of Abraham—that it would be the joining of these two seeds which would bring about a blessing to all nations.

God's plan of redemption was to be progressively expanded until it included anyone from any tribe or nation that desired to return to Him. It began with the making of a covenant with one man, Abraham, and then to the making of a covenant with a whole nation, the natural seed of Abraham. Then, just as He had promised Abraham, He expanded it to include all of the families on the face of the earth. The cross breaks down the barrier and divisions between all people so that anyone may walk through the door of salvation. Jesus is truly the Savior of all of mankind.

It is elementary and well understood by believers that anyone from any nation may now partake of the covenant that leads to salvation. However, many believers still do not understand the role that the Jewish people have in this. They were once separated but are now being grafted back into the root. Many of the growing number of Jewish believers also do not understand this. How are both of these groups now **"fellow members"** and **"fellow partakers"** of the covenant? Do the Jewish converts need to join the church? Or does the church now need to join the Messianic movement?

The answer to this is "neither" and "both." I am not trying to confuse you, but there are aspects of this that are not true, and there are ways in which it is. There is presently a growing controversy about this issue in both camps, which will ultimately lead to searching out these matters until the answers are made clear to both camps. When these answers are made clear they will be the bridge across which both groups begin to relate as they are called—to actually becoming one.

Neither the church nor the Messianic movement is what it is called to be yet. They both need each other for completion. Many still promote what is called "replacement theology" that has the church entirely replacing the Jewish people in God's plan of redemption. Others promote what I call a "replacement, replacement theology," that replaces the church with the Jewish people. Both of these promote a basic misunderstanding of the **"mystery of Christ,"** but in due time it will be made clear.

One thing that is obvious is that the plan of redemption was an unquestionable march toward inclusiveness. God's desire was for even more than all of the families on the face of the earth just being blessed—He **"...desires all men to be saved, and to come to the knowledge of the truth" (I Timothy 2:4).** We should immediately beware of any doctrine that promotes exclusiveness in regard to the covenant. Those who really understand the "mystery" that Paul was writing about will rather promote the fellowship that is required of **"fellow partakers,"** both Jews and Gentiles.

However, unity does not mean conformity. The way I become one with my wife is not by making her into a man, but rather by learning to appreciate and relate to the complimentary differences that God gave to both men and women. The way that this **"mystery of Christ"** is going to be fully understood, and then implemented, is not by making the Jews into Gentiles, or the Gentiles into Jews, but rather by each learning to appreciate and learn from the uniqueness of the other.

Even Peter, who God used to open the door of faith to the Gentiles, had trouble understanding how to relate to the Gentiles. He even had to be publicly rebuked by Paul in Antioch. It seems this is an issue that has yet to be fully resolved by either side. Certainly an entire book would be required to address it adequately. In this study we can do little more than acknowledge that this is one mystery which seems to remain a mystery to most, and yet it must be resolved for either the Jews or the Gentiles to come into their full purpose. For now we understand that we must not embrace doctrines or people who promote exclusivity, or an identity that is according to the flesh rather than by the Spirit. Rather let us endeavor to fulfill the charge of II Corinthians 5:16-21:

> **Therefore from now on we recognize no man according to the flesh; even though we have known Christ according to the flesh, yet now we know Him thus no longer.**
>
> **Therefore if any man is in Christ, he is a new creature; the old things passed away; behold, new things have come.**
>
> **Now all these things are from God, who reconciled us to Himself through Christ, and gave us the ministry of reconciliation,**
>
> **namely, that God was in Christ reconciling the world to Himself, not counting their trespasses against them, and He has committed to us the word of reconciliation.**
>
> **Therefore, we are ambassadors for Christ, as though God were entreating through us; we beg you on behalf of Christ, be reconciled to God.**
>
> **He made Him who knew no sin to be sin on our behalf, that we might become the righteousness of God in Him.**

There is some merit and good that can come from helping people reconcile to their heritage. This is one way we can honor our fathers and mothers. Even so, our goal is not to reconcile people just to their heritage, but to God. We must not allow ourselves to be distracted by those doctrines or people who promote replacing the central purpose of God with an overemphasis of the minor purposes. No one can be fully reconciled to the past, present, or future, if they are not first fully reconciled to God. When that has been accomplished the other issues will be easy.

CHAPTER SEVENTEEN

Power for Grace

We continue our study with three verses that contain both crucial insight into the ministry of Paul, as well as into his heart, Ephesians 3:7-9:

> **I became a servant of this gospel by the gift of God's grace given me through the working of his power.**
>
> **Although I am less than the least of all God's people, this grace was given me: to preach to the Gentiles the unsearchable riches of Christ,**
>
> **and to make plain to everyone the administration of this mystery, which for ages past was kept hidden in God, who created all things (NIV).**

First and foremost, Paul was a servant of the gospel. Everything in his life was focused upon his mission to share the unsearchable riches of Christ. He seemed to walk in continual wonder of God's grace, and his captivation with this one theme pours forth in all of his writings. This passion made the apostle who did not have the privilege of being a disciple of Christ when He walked the earth, possibly the most effective of the apostles. Paul did not walk with the Lord when He was here in the flesh, but few walked with Him more closely in the Spirit. Paul, who had been forgiven so much, seemed to love Him more.

Paul was obviously driven to know the Lord like few have ever been. It was also His passion **"to make plain"** this mystery of God's plan that had been kept hidden until that time. He lived to make known the glory of the One who had captured his own heart. Paul certainly accomplished his purpose. He is without peer as the champion of making the most clear presentation of the gospel of God's grace. He excelled to the point that he may be the most studied author in the world today.

It could be argued that the Epistles of Paul are the most powerful letters ever written. Countless millions have embraced Christ because of the clear exposition of the gospel that is found in these letters. They are forever preserved as canon Scripture. It seems possible, maybe even likely, that no other man or woman of God will have as much fruit in heaven as Paul. Yet, remarkably, he calls himself here **"the least of all God's people."** How could this be?

It was of course the grace of God by which Paul was converted. He was a persecutor of the church, and raged against the saints of God in his youthful zeal. As a Pharisee of Pharisee's, everything in his own reasoning had led him into direct conflict with the truth. Paul knew that he could claim no credit for his apostleship. He owed everything to the grace and mercy of God. This he never forgot, and it is certainly one reason why he is the greatest champion of the gospel of grace to yet walk the earth.

Paul was also one of the most brilliant men of his time, and quite possibly one of the most brilliant men of all time. Yet, he knew profoundly that all of the truth that he possessed he owed to the mercy and grace of God. Man's reasoning can never lead to salvation. Man was given the intelligence to be able to perceive and understand God, but cannot by himself acquire this knowledge—God must reveal Himself if we are going to know Him. Because it was pride that led to the fall of Satan, which released so much evil into creation, it takes humility to begin reversing the fall and opening our hearts back to the blessed Creator. Paul seemed to understand this like few others ever have.

As we read in James 4:6, "**...God is opposed to the proud, but gives grace to the humble.**" In Paul the Lord also demonstrated how even His worst enemies can be welcomed back and helped if they will humble themselves to lay aside their pride. Paul himself is an example of this remarkable grace. Paul walked in God's grace to the end because he never forgot the mercy that God extended to him. Therefore, in genuine humility he really did consider himself the most unworthy of all of the saints. Because of this he credited all that was accomplished through him to God. Therefore, God was able to trust him with extraordinary power for his task.

Interestingly, Paul did not start his ministry quite this humble. Even when he was young and his conversion was still fresh, you can see in the chronology of Paul's letters a progression of humility. In one of his earliest letters, he claims not to be inferior to even the greatest apostles (see II Corinthians 11:5). A few years later this attitude had changed and he called himself "**...the least of the apostles...**" (**I Corinthians 15:9**). In his letter to the Ephesians, Paul goes even further and calls himself the least of the saints (see Ephesians 3:8). In one of his last Epistles, which was written about five years after this one, Paul calls himself "**...the worst of sinners...**" (**I Timothy 1:16** NIV).

Paul truly did labor more than possibly all of the rest of the apostles, and it could possibly be said that he bore the most fruit, and even today may be bearing more fruit than all of the other ministries on the earth combined through his letters. Even so, he actually became more and more humble as he became more and more powerful and fruitful in his labors. This is truly a rare and remarkable example of the truth that with true spiritual maturity there will be increasing humility. It is by the reversal of that which caused the Fall that we are drawn back into an intimate relationship with God.

Again, because God truly does resist the proud and gives His grace to the humble, those who are progressing toward true spiritual maturity, the true grace of God, will also be progressing toward increasing humility. This is all about grace, and therefore those who pursue God's grace do so by pursuing humility. Is this a vision in your life?

One single thing that might radically change our lives would be if, instead of always trying to present a proud and successful image of ourselves, we endeavored to look smaller, devoting ourselves instead to building others up. Over and over we are exhorted in the Scriptures to "humble ourselves." There is not one verse that tells us to exalt ourselves, but rather it makes clear that this is the Lord's job to do this. In Luke 14:11, the Lord stated clearly, **"For everyone who exalts himself will be humbled, and he who humbles himself will be exalted"** (NIV). Do we not have an abundance of examples in our own times of ministries and churches that are built on self-promotion, with all ending up badly?

If we would pray more for others, promote what God is doing through others rather than ourselves, then the Lord would begin to promote us. It is clear that our job is to humble ourselves and it is God's job to do whatever promoting is necessary. If we would live by this, we could be trusted with much more power and true spiritual authority, which would enable us to bear more fruit that would remain.

CHAPTER EIGHTEEN

Witnessing to Principalities

In the last chapter we studied how the mystery of God's grace is revealed through Christ and was made plain through Paul's ministry. The next verse in our study, Ephesians 3:10, adds a significant and remarkable reason why this must be done:

in order that the manifold wisdom of God might now be made known through the church to the rulers and the authorities in the heavenly places.

Most evangelical Christians learn how to witness to other people soon after their conversion, but how many are taught about our calling to be witnesses to principalities and powers **"in the heavenly places?"** How do we do this?

Satan has had a boast since man's fall in the garden. His boast is that even the crowning glory of God's creation, man, given a choice between good and evil, will choose evil. Even after the cross, his boast has continued, declaring that God can choose to forgive men of their evil ways, but He really cannot change them. He even points at the church as proof that given the choice, mankind will choose Satan's ways over God's. Before the end comes, there will be a church without spot or wrinkle, without any corruption in her heart, who will prove for all time, and to all of creation, even to principalities and powers, that good will ultimately prevail over evil.

Presently Satan is still boasting about how even when the first man and woman lived in a perfect world they chose to sin. However, the bride of **"the last Adam,"** the bride of Christ, will live in a most imperfect world, and against all of the opposition of the devil and his hordes, against the opposition of all of fallen mankind, she will choose to obey. She will stand for truth and righteousness without compromise, and she will push the darkness back by the power of the light that she has been given.

When the church finally does this, all of heaven, hell, and earth will look upon the beauty of holiness that is revealed through her. The men of the earth will look upon the men who have been restored to what men were created to be, and they will be drawn to this light, knowing that this is what their nature was meant to be. The women of the world will look upon the dignity, nobility, and grace of the sanctified women of the church, and they will know for certain that this is the way that they too were created to be. Even the principalities and powers will marvel at the grace—the beauty of holiness that is revealed through the church. It will be even more spectacular when this takes place in the darkest times.

This is our calling. The Lord did not die just to save us from the consequences of sin, but from sin itself. If His salvation is continuing to work in our lives, we will be growing up in all things to be like Him. This is one of the central points of the Epistle to the Ephesians, which we will see unfolding more and more as we continue.

It can be easy to be discouraged as we look at a world which is degenerating into increasing darkness, and even the church seems to be doing the same. Even so, you can be sure of one thing. There are thousands upon thousands who are not sliding back into corruption. They are continually growing in the grace and knowledge of the Lord, and their impending revelation to the world will not only stun the world, but will shake the heavens themselves. As the Lord exhorts through Isaiah,

> **"Arise, shine; for your light has come, and the glory of the LORD has risen upon you.**

"For behold, darkness will cover the earth, and deep darkness the peoples; but the LORD will rise upon you, and His glory will appear upon you.

"And nations will come to your light, and kings to the brightness of your rising.

"Lift up your eyes round about, and see; they all gather together, they come to you. Your sons will come from afar, and your daughters will be carried in the arms.

"Then you will see and be radiant, and your heart will thrill and rejoice; because the abundance of the sea will be turned to you, the wealth of the nations will come to you (Isaiah 60:1-5).

The next verse in our study, Ephesians 3:11, states: **"This** (being a witness to principalities) **was in accordance with the eternal purpose which He carried out in Christ Jesus our Lord."** This is obviously an important part of the plan of God, and therefore we must take it very seriously. This should keep us in touch with the perspective that our actions on earth can have significant consequences in the heavenly realm. As we mature in Christ in the spiritual realm, the interaction between earth and heaven should become more and more real to us. However, the most important aspect of this is stated in the next verse, Ephesians 3:12:

in whom we have boldness and confident access through faith in Him.

"Boldness and confident access" to the Father does not mean arrogant access. Our boldness and confidence is always in the blood of Jesus, not our own righteousness. It is not even because of who we are in Christ, but rather in who He is in us. Whenever our boldness is based on our own actions or standing, we are in jeopardy of a terrible fall that is always the result of pride. That is what happened to "the prince of the air," and the evil principalities and powers in the heavenly realm that fell with him. Even so, for us to be of such importance to the Father that we can enter boldly into His presence at will, and yet remain humble, always acknowledging that our righteousness and standing before Him is by the blood of Jesus alone, is also a witness to the principalities and powers. It is also true that because our boldness and confidence is in the cross, we will be even more bold and confident than if we are trying to stand on our own righteousness or strength.

This is where we need to separate pride from faith, and true humility from false humility. Pride is focused on ourselves, what we have done, or who we think we are. Faith is always focused on God, what He has done and who He is. When God is the source of our boldness and confidence, it will never be arrogant. This is why we are told in I Corinthians 13:4-5, **"Love is patient, love is kind, and is not jealous; love does not brag and is not arrogant, does not act unbecomingly; it does not seek its own..."**

This is why true Christian maturity is reflected by boldness and confidence in all things that can be incomprehensible to those who do not know the Lord, and yet this boldness has all of the grace and dignity of true humility that is not self-seeking, arrogant, or presumptuous. How could anyone who has truly beheld the cross not be humbled before it? How could anyone who has beheld who He now is, and where He now sits above all authority and dominion, not be humbled before Him? If He who dwelt in such glory would so humble Himself to become a man for us, not to mention suffering what He did at the hands of men, how could we fail to be even more humble? We are humbled because He truly is worthy of all honor, glory, and dominion. For us to presume that we are deserving of any in comparison is a terrible and base delusion, but we are emboldened because He loved us that much!

We have **"boldness and confident access"** to the Father also because we know that He loves us. This sounds elementary, but many Christians have a concept of the Father as being the God of the Old Testament who would have long ago destroyed us if it were not for the atonement of the cross. In this we forget that it was the Father who so loved the world that He sent His only begotten Son for our salvation. Jesus perfectly reflected the Father while on the earth. All of the compassion that He had for sinners and the oppressed is a direct reflection of the compassion that the Father has for us. God is love, and because of His love we can come boldly before Him and know that He will not only accept us, but desire for us to draw closer to Him.

When we perceive His love, and the completeness of the atonement to cover our transgressions, we can come before the Lord with the same boldness regardless of how good or bad we have been. We are not coming on our own righteousness; His sacrifice was enough to pay for even our worst sin. Therefore, we learn to run to Him when we sin, not away from Him. Only from Him can we receive the grace that we need.

The ultimate strength of every Christian will be determined by our willingness to use the access that we have been given to the throne of God. It is here that the truth we have believed becomes the life that we live. We begin by coming for the grace that we need. We then learn to go for the needs of others. As we grow we will start coming to Him just to be with Him. Remember that we do not have to wait to be mature or perfect to come before Him, but we mature and are perfected by coming before Him.

Because even the Son of God came as One who is **"...gentle and humble in heart..." (Matthew 11:29)** one of the greatest witnesses to all, even to principalities and powers, is to walk in the power and authority of such a high calling as to be sons and daughters of God, joint heirs with the King of kings, and yet remain humble. Nothing may be a greater witness that redemption has truly accomplished its purpose in our lives than the restoration of our relationship to God and one another.

CHAPTER NINETEEN

Tribulations and Glory

Now we proceed to Ephesians 3:13, which has proven hard to understand for many modern, western Christians:

"Therefore I ask you not to lose heart at my tribulations on your behalf, for they are your glory."

It is understandable that Paul would ask the Ephesians **"not to lose heart"** when they see their apostle suffering tribulations. The big question is how is Paul suffering on behalf of the Ephesian Christians, and for their glory? The answer to this is in Acts 14: 21-22, which is written about Paul's missionary journey:

And after they had preached the gospel to that city and had made many disciples, they returned to Lystra and to Iconium and to Antioch,

strengthening the souls of the disciples, encouraging them to continue in the faith, and saying, "Through many tribulations we must enter the kingdom of God."

Paul knew that the tribulations that he was going through were for the purpose of providing an entry for him into the kingdom. Tribulations are a door to the kingdom. They force us to go to the cross, and as we do this, dying to our own self-will, the Lord is able to trust us with more authority. This would mean nothing less than more of the glory of God being manifested through him, and his ministry, including the Ephesians.

Remember when Moses asked to see the glory of the Lord? The Lord told him that he could not see His face, but He would show Moses His back, which He did (see Exodus 33:13-23). Why would He show Moses His back in order to reveal His glory? What did Moses see on His back? He saw His stripes. How could this be, since the Lord was not to be crucified for another thousand years? Remember, His works were finished before the foundation of the world (see Hebrews 4:3). The glory of God is much more than beautiful colors. There is nothing in all of eternity that will portray the glory of God like His suffering on our behalf. That is why when Moses asked to see His glory He showed him His back.

The same is true of us. That is why when Paul's apostolic authority was challenged he pointed to his afflictions, not his works, as evidence of his authority (see II Corinthians 11:23-27). This is why the original twelve rejoiced when they were beaten for preaching the gospel. Acts 5:41 states: **"So they went on their way from the presence of the Council, rejoicing that they had been considered worthy to suffer shame for His name."**

That is why Paul went about "encouraging the saints" by telling them that they would enter the kingdom through tribulations. Today many could hardly think of anything more discouraging! This is because so few today understand true spiritual authority, and the unfathomable privilege it is to ever be considered worthy to suffer for the sake of the gospel.

Christ Jesus is our example. Where would we be if He had avoided the cross? It was by His enduring the cross that the ultimate victory over evil has been accomplished. We too have been told to take up our crosses daily, to lay down our own lives, and that this is the true and only path to glory and fulfillment. As the Lord Jesus Himself made clear to us in Matthew 16:25, **"For whoever wishes to save his life shall lose it; but whoever loses his life for My sake shall find it."**

In Romans 5:3-5 Paul elaborates on this, saying, **"...but we also exult in our tribulations, knowing that tribulation brings**

about perseverance; and perseverance, proven character; and proven character, hope; and hope does not disappoint, because the love of God has been poured out within our hearts through the Holy Spirit who was given to us." Paul's tribulations that the Ephesians observed were an example of Paul himself embracing this basic Christian truth.

It is a false doctrine that is in basic conflict with the Scriptures which teaches that Jesus went to the cross and suffered so that we do not have to. He did not go to the cross and suffer so that we would not have to suffer, but rather so we could be victorious in our suffering. In fact, we can be so victorious that we begin to **"exult in our tribulations,"** seeing them as the great opportunities they are to triumph over evil. If this is not true, what about the martyrs? Did they die needlessly? Of course not. We need to understand that many today are preaching "another gospel," a gospel that is truly an enemy of the cross. This has been the case since the first century. It is nothing new, but if we are going to walk in truth we must face even the most difficult biblical truths with a determination to receive them as they are, not as we may want them to be.

In Jeremiah 17:10 we read, **"I, the LORD, search the heart, I test the mind, even to give to each man according to his ways, according to the results of his deeds."** In Jeremiah 20:12 he says, **"Yet, O LORD of hosts, Thou who dost test the righteous..."** God's tests do not come because we have done something wrong, but because we are doing something right.

Every trial is a test. A test is different from a temptation. Just as our tests in school were given so that we could pass and go on to higher grades, spiritual tests are given to us so that we can go on to greater anointing and spiritual authority. That is why Paul wrote to the Ephesians that they should be encouraged by his tribulations, and see them as being for their glory. He was in a sense saying, "Look at the great tests I have been given! What opportunities! We are really going to see glory from these, which you will share in because you stand so united with me in my purpose."

As my friend Francis Frangipane likes to say, "You never fail one of God's tests, you just keep taking them until you pass." This is true. This is called going in circles in the wilderness. We must stop running from trials and begin to embrace them as the opportunities that they are. They are going to come anyway, so why not make use of them? It is by embracing and overcoming them that we will enter into the kingdom.

An army is not raised in order to run from battles, but to win them. Without a battle there can be no victory. Battles are coming, but we have the encouragement of II Corinthians 2:14 that He "**...always leads us in His triumph in Christ, and manifests through us the sweet aroma of the knowledge of Him in every place.**" Battles are a lot more fun when you know that you can't lose! That's the truth that we need to seize and walk in. Then we will truly exult and glory during tribulations in expectation of the great victories we will experience.

The title that God uses more than any other in Scripture is "**the Lord of hosts,**" or "**the Lord of armies.**" This title is actually used about ten times more than any other of His titles. How many generals do you know from history who never fought a battle? Just as all of the great generals are known for their performance in battle, all great Christians will be known in eternity for the same.

CHAPTER TWENTY

Family and the Inner Man

In this chapter we will look at the next three verses, Ephesians 3:14-16:

For this reason, I bow my knees before the Father,

from whom every family in heaven and on earth derives its name,

that He would grant you, according to the riches of His glory, to be strengthened with power through His Spirit in the inner man.

It is interesting that Paul would bring up how every family in heaven and earth derives its name from God the Father. This indicates that there are families in heaven just as there are on the earth. We also know from Genesis how the Lord ordained families, and that families would become nations. He also gave His promises to families, not just individuals. We also see a great deal of emphasis being given to the genealogies in Scripture, indicating the emphasis that the Lord gives to our family lineage.

Family relationships are obviously very important to the Lord. This is why it is also obvious that one of the devil's top priorities is to assault families, and if possible, even tear down the very family structure. This is something that we have covered in some depth before, but must always keep in mind. Our families must be given the priority that God gives to them. If we fail with our family, we have truly failed in a significant way in this life.

This is not to say that if we have failed in family relationships in the past that we cannot be restored and succeed in the future. Even God is divorced, as we read in Jeremiah where He gave Israel a certificate of divorce. Even so, there are few things that we can do that will be more pleasing to the Lord, and do more to resist the devil, than to strengthen our families.

As one friend of mine, Dr. John Chacha has noted, we are spending great amounts of time and money to save every obscure species on the planet, but little is being done to save that which is possibly the most threatened species of all—the male. Manhood is now under possibly the greatest onslaught of all from the devil and his hosts. Men, and especially fathers, are attacked as buffoons in almost every sitcom. There is a continual attempt made to blur the differences between men and women in books, movies, and even textbooks. This is because God is the Father, and there is no higher calling than fatherhood because this is the one office that we can share with Him.

Motherhood is likewise under an unrelenting assault because no one can become a father without a mother being present. The church is the bride, the wife of the Son of God, and is called to be the spiritual mother of His children. The father may be the head of the family but the mother is the center and hub around which family life revolves. The mother is the one who carries the life, gives birth, nurtures, protects, and helps to mature the emerging ones, the heirs. Mothers are the most important teachers of all, which is why Solomon, the wisest man who lived, after writing his proverbs of wisdom stated that these were the things that his mother taught him! (see Proverbs 31). Even though he was the son of King David, one of the greatest kings to ever live, he admitted to having received his crown from his mother (see Song of Solomon 3:11).

To esteem fathers in their place is not to in any way belittle mothers and their place, but rather to establish it. Just as the Lord laid down His life for His bride, fathers exercise their authority in the family out of service to the family. The Lord also made men and women different for a reason—we have different roles and to blur these differences is to begin a fundamental breakdown of the family itself, which has obviously been a high agenda of the devil from the beginning.

In the last verse of our study in this chapter we see that the Lord wants to strengthen us with His **"power, through His Spirit in the inner man,"** which He does according to His riches in glory. This indicates the value that the Lord puts on the strengthening of our inner man. What would happen if we started doing the same? How different would most of us be if we just spent as much time cleaning up, beautifying, and feeding our heart as we did our body?

It is a good thing to see so many gyms and health clubs springing up everywhere, and I could personally stand to spend more time in one. Even so, we will be much better off if we spent more time building up our inner man than the outer. The outer man is going to deteriorate at some point regardless of how much effort we put into building it up, but our inner man is going to last forever. As this verse states, the Lord has invested **"the riches of His glory"** in our inner man, so how much more value should we give to it?

I would much rather be able to heal someone of cancer, or be used to enable a cripple to walk, than be able to run a little farther, or lift a little more weight. Faith, which all of the gifts of the Spirit operate by, in some ways operates like our muscles. The more you use faith, the larger and more powerful it becomes. In natural training for the body, you do not get stronger until you work past the point that you did previously. We should have similar goals for our faith.

I had a dream in which the Lord told me He wanted me to move literal mountains with my faith. He was not talking about mountains of problems, or obstacles, but mountains such as Everest. In this dream I started with furniture, and grew until I could move cars, literally see them picked up and moved through the air with a word. I grew in this faith until I could literally say to a mountain **"...be taken up and cast into the sea..."** (Matthew 21:21) and it obeyed me.

I do understand that cults and those involved in the black arts do levitation as a part of their craft, but that does not nullify what the Lord Jesus Himself said about us being able to move a mountain with faith as small as a mustard seed. In fact, I was shown that we would have to have this kind of faith in the last days. I want to have the kind of faith that can say to SARS, or the ebola virus, "Don't come near these shores," and turn it back.

For us to get to this place we actually need spiritual gyms, which is in fact what the church is called to be. It is good to be in good shape physically, but far more important to be in shape spiritually. Peter Lord once said, "The main thing is to keep the main thing the main thing."

CHAPTER TWENTY-ONE

The Knowledge of Life

The verses that we will study in this chapter are Ephesians 3:17-19:

so that Christ may dwell in your hearts through faith; and that you, being rooted and grounded in love,

may be able to comprehend with all the saints what is the breadth and length and height and depth,

and to know the love of Christ which surpasses knowledge, that you may be filled up to all the fulness of God.

This states that we keep Christ in our hearts by believing in Him. Does this mean the more faith we have in Him the more He dwells in us? That seems incomprehensible to some because they try to relate spiritual realities to physical ones, and they do not always relate.

In the book of Acts, we see the disciples being baptized in the Holy Spirit, and then we see them being "filled with the Spirit" (see Acts 2:4) again at different times. Were they being baptized in the Spirit repeatedly? Did the Spirit leak out of them somehow? Again, when we try to understand these things in terms of the way we understand things in the natural, they may not make sense to us, but they are written because they are spiritual truths that we need to understand.

Christ does dwell or occupy our hearts through faith. The more we believe in Him, the more He will take over our hearts. If we start giving much more attention to something else, then it will start to occupy our hearts in place of Christ. Therefore, it should be our goal every day to see the Lord more clearly, to be more occupied with Him so that He will more fully occupy our hearts. Then the next crucial truth that this text addresses will become a reality to us—we will become **"rooted and grounded in love."** We do this because **"God is love,"** (**I John 4:8**) and if He is abiding in our hearts He will always lead us to love.

It is noteworthy here that he does not say "rooted and grounded in sound doctrine." Sound doctrine is important, but what really establishes us in Christ is love. As Paul stated so wonderfully in I Corinthians 13, we can have all knowledge, and even all faith so as to remove mountains, but if we do not have love it has profited us nothing! Think about that. Should we not therefore pursue love above all things? The way we pursue love is by pursuing God who is love.

As this text declares, it is as we are **"rooted and grounded in love"** that we come to know the **"breadth, and length and height and depth."** We might rephrase this accurately to say, "it is by love that we come to know anything." If love is not the foundation of our knowledge then the knowledge we have will not be accurate. Anything but love distorts knowledge.

We will not be able to really know a person until we love that person. Anything but love will cause us to misunderstand them. If you love someone you will tend to see them more deeply than you would otherwise. Likewise, we will not be able to really know a country until we love that country. If we love a country we will be compelled to understand it more. We will not be able to know any subject with much depth until we love that subject. You will never know height and depth of math until you begin to love math. You will never know history rightly until you begin to love history. Love draws us past the superficial. Therefore, love is the foundation of true knowledge that is compelled to go higher, deeper, and further.

It is in this way that we are led by the Lord in our studies. In school there were many things that I had to learn to get by, but if I did not love those subjects I would learn just enough to get by, and probably have not used that knowledge much since. However, the things that I love I continue to pursue. This is why Jesus said living waters come from our **"innermost being," (John 7:38)** or our heart. Therefore what is life to you will be what you care the deepest about. It is in this way that we should be led through life by love.

Those who are led by love will never be superficial. Love compels you to know the depth, height, width, and breadth. Love compels us to go further. That is why we read in the next verse that the **"love of Christ...surpasses knowledge,"** and it is by His love that we are **"filled up to all the fulness of God."** If we are being led through life by a love for God, we will continually be drawn to Him until we know His fullness. This text implies that we can actually know Him that well.

Does this mean we can know everything that there is to know about God? This is not what this text is saying. For example, I can drink ocean water until I am filled with it, but this does not mean that the whole ocean is in me. We can become filled with God or know the fullness of God as much as is humanly possible, but this does not mean that all of God is in us. However, those who are filled with God are going to know everything else with greater depth, breadth, etc., than they could otherwise.

Of course, our love for God should surpass all other loves in our lives. If we are led through life by our love for Christ, we will have a life that greatly transcends just having knowledge—it will be a life that is filled with life because it is filled with love. Love is the foundation of true knowledge, and is the path of life.

So why not determine to go to work today filled with love for God, and the love of God, so we can love all that we come in contact with, and so we can even love our jobs. If we will do this we will be amazed at how we see and understand everything much better than we ever have before. We will also be filled with life that touches and awakens others to the true love of God.

CHAPTER TWENTY-TWO

The Abundance of Christ Within

W̲e have been going through Ephesians verse by verse because it is this Epistle, more than any other, that reveals the heart of Paul's revelation of the glorious calling of the church. This is what he again calls us to know in the verses we will examine in this chapter, Ephesians 3:20-21:

Now to Him who is able to do exceeding abundantly beyond all that we ask or think, according to the power that works within us,

to Him be the glory in the church and in Christ Jesus to all generations forever and ever. Amen.

I have never met any Christian who was not sure that the Lord could in fact do much more for them than they could ever ask or think—they just were not sure if He would. This is a valid question. It is apparent that the Lord has never done all that He could. The Lord could have healed every sick person in the world, and provided more than enough food for all of the hungry, etc. There is no limit to what He can do, but He has limited what He will do until certain conditions are met.

The conditions that God has placed on the release of His works are mostly related to faith and obedience. However, the second part of the verse above is crucial to understanding the release of God's power, and it is often overlooked. His abundance

107

is related to **"the power that works within us."** He does not just want to reveal His power to us, but through us. This is not to make us egocentric. But because it has been His ultimate purpose to make man His dwelling place, He wants to reveal Himself through His people.

This has been to date the best reason for people not to believe in the Lord. Even so, by the end of this age it will be the best reason to believe in Him. Most Christians understand the purpose of the Lord in revealing Himself through His people, but many have one major misunderstanding that hinders the practical outworking of this great truth. This misunderstanding is the wrong teaching that "God does not exalt men." The Scriptures tell us repeatedly that He does. In fact, He promises that **"...whoever humbles himself shall be exalted" (Matthew 23:12).**

Have you ever noticed that those who emphasize the most that "God does not exalt men" can be some of the most arrogant people of all? They reveal their pride by becoming judges of everyone else, especially those who they perceive to be exalting themselves. Self-promotion is one of the most destructive factors to a true ministry, and the Lord also promises to humble everyone who exalts himself, but we need to let Him do this or we will fall into a deadly trap. I have never read a Scripture that says "Humble your neighbor," or one that encourages us to humble those who are exalting themselves. For us to set ourselves up as judges, or to consider it our job to humble others, is one of the most arrogant things we can do, because we are doing the very thing, we are judging in others.

Idealism is a form of humanism, and the ideals of humility are usually very far from the character that God is seeking in us. David was perceived by his brothers as being arrogant when he refused to be intimidated by Goliath. True faith is usually perceived as arrogance by those who are trapped in the delusions of false humility.

We will never be worthy of anything that we received from the Lord because of our own goodness or righteousness. However, to feel unworthy is self-centeredness, the root of self-righteousness. We are still only looking to ourselves instead of to the One who is our righteousness. The Lord said to "agree with your enemy," so whenever the enemy tells me that I am not good enough for the Lord to use me, I agree with him. However, I know that I am not my righteousness, and my righteousness will never be the reason why the Lord uses me. It is by having the humility to trust in Him and the power of His cross that enables Him to do His works through us.

It is foolish for us to consider ourselves as great because the Lord does great works through us. As someone once said, it is like the donkey that Jesus was riding into Jerusalem, thinking that all of those Hosannas were for him instead of the One who was riding on his back. Even so, the Lord is going to reveal His glory and His power through His people. We will never be worthy of this. We will never be able to earn it. All we can do is believe God. If we believe Him, we will also obey Him. That is all we can do, but it is also all that we have to do.

PART IV

Built for Eternity

A Study of Ephesians
Chapter 4

CHAPTER TWENTY-THREE

A Worthy Walk

I n this chapter we begin our study of possibly the most practical and concise chapters in the Scriptures for revealing the high calling and purpose of the church, and how to get there— Ephesians 4. Before continuing in our study of this remarkable and revolutionary chapter, it would be good to review how Paul laid the foundation for what he wrote in Ephesians.

There is a pattern in Paul's letters and it is followed in this one too. The first part is usually a salutation and then a reminder of some of the general principles of the faith. Then he boldly declares the main purpose for the letter concisely and powerfully. Paul did not waste many words. He then finishes with encouragement for the saints to arise and finish the work that they have been called to do. This chapter contains the heart of his message in this Epistle to the Ephesians, stated with characteristic boldness and clarity. In relation to the church's purpose on the earth, this chapter is probably the most important in the Bible. We will begin our study of it with verses 1-3:

> **I, therefore, the prisoner of the Lord, entreat you to walk in a manner worthy of the calling with which you have been called,**
>
> **with all humility and gentleness, with patience, showing forbearance to one another in love,**

being diligent to preserve the unity of the Spirit in the bond of peace.

Paul wrote this letter while he was a prisoner in Rome not long before his execution. It is noteworthy that he did not consider himself a prisoner of the Romans, but a **"prisoner of the Lord."** Those who live by faith know that nothing can happen to them that the Lord does not allow for His own reasons. Therefore, Paul accepted his situation as ordained by God. Living by this faith is the only way we will be able to walk in a manner worthy of our calling.

Those who walk in faith are always free even if they are in the strongest prison. Paul did not fear death because he died daily. He was already dead to this world, so there was really nothing that the world could do to him to steal his true life. Those who walk in this manner, in the true faith of God, will be the most free, bold, resolute, joyful, humble, and gracious people who walk the earth. By his own admission, Paul was more at home in the Spirit and with the Lord than he was in the body anyway, so when they took his body it meant little to him. When it's time to go, that's the way we should all be—ready.

The way Paul encouraged the Ephesians to **"walk in a manner worthy"** of the Lord was to walk in humility, gentleness, and showing patience and forbearance to one another in love. Christians should walk in a dignity and nobility that exceeds that of any earthly royalty. We are the children of the King of kings. If you have ever beheld someone of a truly noble spirit, you will always find these qualities. One who knows who they are, and knows that they are doing the will of God, will have a strength and boldness that allows them to be humble, gentle, patient, as well as showing forbearance and love. Have you ever seen one who was impatient in a noble spirit?

Then Paul charges his readers to be **"diligent to preserve the unity of the Spirit in the bond of peace."** This is something that requires much diligence because the primary assault of the devil against the church is intended to cause divisions. There are times when a church may need to divide for strategic reasons—such as sending some out to new areas, but this kind will always be done with vision and purpose, in the bond of peace. Therefore, we should view all other divisions as the work of the devil.

It is for this reason that Paul wrote in Romans 16:17 to **"mark them which cause divisions and offences contrary to the doctrine which ye have learned; and avoid them"** (KJV). Those who cause divisions in the church may strongly assert that they are sent by the Lord, and even believe it. But these are the devil's messengers who must be detected and marked as such, if we are going to avoid the damage that they have been sent to do.

The devil seems to understand better than most Christians that unity brings a multiplication of authority. As we are told in Deuteronomy 32:30, one can chase a thousand but two will put ten thousand to flight. The Lord said in Matthew 18:19, **"...if two of you agree on earth about anything that they may ask, it shall be done for them by My Father who is in heaven."** The word that is translated **"agree"** here means a bit more than just intellectually assenting to a matter together—it reveals the tremendous potential power of unity. If we understand this, how can we not be most diligent to preserve the unity of the Spirit?

In Genesis 11:6 we have a most remarkable statement by the Lord: **"And the LORD said, "Behold, they are one people, and they all have the same language. And this is what they began to do, and now nothing which they purpose to do will be impossible for them."** Unity releases a force beyond what most Christians understand. If this could be said of those who were trying to build the Tower of Babel, how much more true is it of those who have been sanctified and are doing the will of the Lord?

Before the Lord does any great work He looks for a people in unity that He can work through. We see this in the book of Acts and throughout history. The people do not have to be many if they are in unity. Francis Frangipane likes to say, "In the Lord, four of a kind beats a full house."

Without question, those who are doing the Lord's work will always promote unity and fight division. On the night before He was crucified, in what must be the greatest prayer in Scripture to reveal the heart of God, the Lord prayed repeatedly for the unity of His people (see John 17). Those who have His heart will have the same devotion. Unity is crucial if we are going to rise to fulfill our high calling in Christ.

CHAPTER TWENTY-FOUR

Growing in Unity

In this chapter we will study the simple, but essential truth that we began discussing in the last chapter about the importance of unity in the work of God, which Paul elaborates on in Ephesians 4:4-6:

> **There is one body and one Spirit, just as also you were called in one hope of your calling;**
>
> **one Lord, one faith, one baptism,**
>
> **one God and Father of all who is over all and through all and in all.**

Unity is a basic characteristic of the Godhead, and of those who are sent to do the work of God. The universe was created to fit together in a profound and glorious harmony. There is a harmony and symmetry to all that God does. What He creates always comes from unity and proceeds toward unity. The unifying force in all that He does is the Son, as we see in Colossians 1:16-17:

> **For by Him all things were created, both in the heavens and on earth, visible and invisible, whether thrones or dominions or rulers or authorities—all things have been created by Him and for Him.**
>
> **And He is before all things, and in Him all things hold together.**

Jesus is the One that everything was made through and for. In everything that was created, the Father was looking for the likeness of His Son. He is looking for His Son in us. As we are told Ephesians 1:9-10, Jesus is the mystery of God's will, and the ultimate goal of all that was created is to be summed up in Him. Therefore, the ultimate goal of our life and everything that we are doing should be to abide in Him and be found in Him. In this way He is the unifying force behind all of creation.

It is the devil that brought the corruption of division and disunity. Therefore, it is easy to recognize the work of each. One proceeds toward unity and harmony—the other toward division. We might also recognize the work of the Lord and the schemes of the devil in our own life by the same. Where is the unity, harmony, and peace? What is the source of discord? The Lord is always moving us toward harmony and peace, and the enemy's most basic strategy against us is to bring divisions. This we are told in Jude when he warned about the "fault-finders" and "mockers" who would come in the last days. **These are the ones who cause divisions, worldly-minded, devoid of the Spirit" (Jude 19).**

Even so, we must understand that the Lord will sometimes bring the sword of division as He stated in Matthew 10:34-36:

> **"Do not think that I came to bring peace on the earth; I did not come to bring peace, but a sword.**
>
> **"For I came to set a man against his father, and a daughter against her mother, and a daughter-in-law against her mother-in-law;**
>
> **and a man's enemies will be the members of his household."**

The Lord will sometimes bring about temporary division so that He can bring an ultimate unity. He does this because the ultimate peace requires the tearing down of evil strongholds and fortresses that exalt themselves against the truth.

We might also discern the work of the enemy by the ultimate outcome of a matter, and can be fooled if we look only at the interim steps. The enemy will use a temporary unity to bring about a much more devastating division later. The devil has many alliances that have the appearance of unity. However, we can always discern if something is from God or not by whether the ultimate goal is Christ. If it is, then the steps toward that ultimate goal will draw us ever closer to Him.

As we proceed toward the goal of Christlikeness, we will always find more unity, harmony, and peace within our own hearts. Even if our unity with Him creates discord with those who do not serve Him, there is no greater harmony and peace that we can ever know than being one with Him. If we are abiding in Him, we will also sow the seeds of unity, harmony, and peace everywhere. This is how we discern the wisdom that is from above, as we read in James 3:17-18:

But the wisdom from above is first pure, then peaceable, gentle, reasonable, full of mercy and good fruits, unwavering, without hypocrisy.

And the seed whose fruit is righteousness is sown in peace by those who make peace.

For this reason let us heed the exhortation of I Corinthians 1:10, **"Now I exhort you, brethren, by the name of our Lord Jesus Christ, that you all agree, and there be no divisions among you, but you be made complete in the same mind and in the same judgment."** As we stated in the last chapter, we must beware of and even **"...mark them which cause divisions..." (Romans 16:17** KJV) so as not to associate with them. Those whose works cause divisions instead of unity are walking contrary to Christ.

CHAPTER TWENTY-FIVE

Your Free Gift

In the last chapter we looked at the critical truth that is revealed in Ephesians 4:4-6 regarding unity. In those verses, we were not just called to unity, but were told that we have unity in Christ. If we are abiding in Him, we will have unity with one another because how can a body be divided against itself? As we look at verses 7 and 8 in this chapter, we are given another crucial element of true church life:

> **But to each one of us grace was given according to the measure of Christ's gift.**
>
> **Therefore it says, "When He ascended on high, He led captive a host of captives, and He gave gifts to men."**

To **"each one"** was given a measure of Christ's gift. We are all members of Christ's body, and all have a specific function in it. If any part of the body does not function for a long period of time it will become atrophied. This is another one of the simple truths that has been one of the most elusive for the church.

For several years I have tried to ask every large church and every large conference at which I spoke, how many of the believers present knew their gifts and ministries in the body of Christ. The results were actually much worse than I anticipated. Only about 5 percent were able to positively answer that they even knew their own gifts and ministry in the body of Christ, and only about half of those were actually functioning in their gifts. Consider how well you would be doing if less than 5 percent of your body was functioning! That is the present condition of the body of Christ.

This is certainly one reason for the weakness and ineffectiveness of the church. Part of the problem is the structure of the church that has evolved. It is now mostly a spectator sport with a few people doing the ministry and the rest cheering them on while passively sitting in their seats. New Testament church life is meant to be much more than this, and it will be before the end of this age comes. The Lord will have a fully functioning body that has all of the grace, dignity, and power of the most fully developed human body. We can count on this because our God finishes what He begins, and this was His expressed purpose for His church.

So how do we get from where we are to where we are called to be? The rest of this chapter in Ephesians will give us some crucial insights into this, but these verses are foundational to understanding. When the Lord ascended, He gave gifts to men. He is giving Himself when He gives these gifts. That is why we are each given grace according to the measure of Christ's gift.

I have heard many teach that we should not seek the gifts but rather the Giver. This sounds glib and wise, but it is actually contrary to Scripture. In I Corinthians 12-14, we are exhorted to pursue spiritual gifts, and especially the best ones. What such teachers fail to realize is that one of the ways we seek the Lord is by seeking His gifts. The gifts are Him. When He walked the earth, He exhibited every one of the gifts of the Spirit. When He ascended, He began giving these gifts, which are a basic part of His nature to men.

It is by growing in the gifts of the Spirit that we actually grow up into Christ, abide in Him, and become like Him. All of His gifts are love gifts, and as we will view later, are actually founded upon the fruit of the Spirit. He heals because He loves and does not want people to suffer. When this gift begins to grow in you, it is because you begin to identify with His love and compassion for people that are sick. Likewise, when we grow in the gift of prophecy it is because we begin to see with His eyes, hear with His ears, and feel with His heart. When we grow in the gift of miracles we begin to identify with His power, and since He is the Almighty, we must know His power to really know Him. As we see the way He uses His power through us, we begin to understand His ways in this, and grow up into Him.

So we are not just seeking gifts for the sake of seeking gifts, but we are seeking the Lord Himself. This also works together with the verses we covered in the last chapter about unity. This is because no one person is given all of His gifts, and therefore all of Him. It is therefore only as we come together that He can be fully manifested in our midst. This we also see in I Corinthians 1:4-7:

> **I thank my God always concerning you, for the grace of God which was given you in Christ Jesus,**
>
> **that in everything you were enriched in Him, in all speech and all knowledge,**
>
> **even as the testimony concerning Christ was confirmed in you,**
>
> **so that you are not lacking in any gift...**

The **"testimony concerning Christ was confirmed"** in them because they were **"not lacking in any gift."** When all of the gifts are functioning in the body, then the Lord is fully functioning in the body. Then He can do all that He wants to do through us. This is what He wants to do through every local church. He wants to be able to manifest Himself through us in all of the ways that He manifests Himself to men through every local church. However, this will never happen until all of the members are equipped and in unity, functioning together. How we get from where we are now to where we are supposed to be is the message of the rest of Ephesians, which will be our focus over the next chapters as we proceed in our study.

CHAPTER TWENTY-SIX

Being Filled

In this chapter we will proceed to cover Ephesians 4:9-10, which ties together even more firmly the message of the verses that we have studied in the last two chapters.

Now this expression, "He ascended," what does it mean except that He also had descended into the lower parts of the earth?

He who descended is Himself also He who ascended far above all the heavens, that He might fill all things.

Jesus has ascended and is again sitting at His Father's right hand in all of the glory and splendor of the Godhead. For us to fully comprehend this fact we must also understand why He **"descended into the lower parts of the earth."** He became a peasant in the most despised town in the most despised nation on earth because of His love for us. This will be one of the great manifestations of His nature for the creation to behold throughout eternity. To just ponder this one truth will be enough to occupy us for millions of years!

There are no human words adequate for describing the revelation of God's nature revealed by what He did for us. Anyone who truly beholds His life on the earth and the cross, should never again be in doubt about one thing—God loves us! This is repeated so much because it is a basic understanding that we must have in our heart if we are going to fulfill our purpose in Him. We are called to do all things for the purpose of His kingdom, but all of the things that He called us to do are also the things which are best for us. He loves us like the most loving father because He is our Father and His basic nature is love.

We must also understand that the reason He descended to become a man and live among us was so that when He prevailed and ascended **"He might fill all things."** As we covered previously, the ultimate purpose of God in the creation is that all things might be summed up in His Son (see Ephesians 1:10). As we proceed to examine the calling upon the church, how He designed it, and what it is to become, we must always keep in mind that the church is the primary vehicle through which God intends to reconcile the world to Himself.

Therefore, our success as a church will be determined by how we are used to reconcile those within our sphere of authority back to God. He wants to use His church to begin this process so that He will again **"fill all things."** How are we being used to fill our neighborhoods with Him? Our jobs? Our cities? Our nations? This is our basic purpose for being here.

Of course, we will only be effective in this to the degree that we allow Him to fill us. This will be directly reflected in the way that He fills our time and our mind—our consciousness. The Lord lives in us. Did we wake up this morning in His presence? Did we go to work in close fellowship with Him? If not, we woke up in a delusion, a deception. We let the lower things cloud our perception of Him. The greatest truth, the only true reality, is God. If He actually lives in us, how can anything else steal our attention from Him?

Solomon built the most glorious temple ever constructed for God. However, when God filled that temple, no one's attention was on the temple! They were captured by the One who was filling it. If there is too much attention on the temple, it can only be because God is not in it.

The church is a wonderful and glorious creation, but our goal for building the church is so the manifest presence of the

Lord will come. God is what we signed up for, not the church. The church is a blessing, and will become the most compelling society on earth, but it is only a shadow of the reality of heaven that we are called to represent. The greatest reality of heaven is the presence of the Lord.

So how does this practically work out in our lives? We have jobs to do. We have to feed this body hamburgers and they cost money! We need houses, cars, and things so we can function in this modern world. All of this may be true, and the Lord is not opposed to our having these things, but if Christ is not more important, and more real than all of these other things, then our life is full of idols.

Lukewarmness is the worst state that any Christian can ever fall into. The reason for the lukewarmness of the Laodicean church is that they had everything they needed. Things really can be the greatest distraction from our ultimate purpose. God loves to give His children good things, and He commanded much more feasting than fasting, but we must guard our hearts against idols, even those things that have been given to us by God.

Asceticism is not the answer to our idolatry. That quickly becomes a measure of our own righteousness in place of the cross. The Lord does not necessarily want us to love anyone or anything less than we do—He just wants us to love Him more. He wants us to love Him so much that He can give us all things, but we must not be distracted by them because He is far greater than anything created.

There is no greater treasure than our salvation and the fellowship that we can now have with God, which results because He descended all the way to the cross for us. Therefore, let us voluntarily go to the cross every day, willingly offering all that we are and have. Let us be committed every day to the reality that our days are only going to be successful if we do His will. When He is the One who fills our lives, He can trust us with all things, but we have a much greater purpose than just gaining stuff. When He fills our lives, He will overflow through us, bringing salvation to others, and then He will begin to fill them too.

This is why the most clear and succinct declaration of the ultimate apostolic mandate is found in Galatians 4:19 when Paul said, **"My children, with whom I am again in labor until Christ is formed in you..."** The true success of any ministry, or any church, will be by how it brought forth the formation of Christ within His people. Are the people in our church becoming like Him? That should always be the ultimate test of our success.

Jesus ascended so that He can fill all things, and it is by our ascending with Him that He begins to fill our lives. The cross is the foundation of knowing God, but He is no longer on the cross. He has ascended, and if we are going to abide in Him now, it must be by sitting with Him on His throne. Our goal now must be that He *fills* our lives.

CHAPTER TWENTY-SEVEN

Being Equipped

O ur text for this chapter has become one of the most often quoted, and to some, the most controversial Scriptures in recent times, Ephesians 4:11-13:

And He gave some as apostles, and some as prophets, and some as evangelists, and some as pastors and teachers,

for the equipping of the saints for the work of service, to the building up of the body of Christ;

until we all attain to the unity of the faith, and of the knowledge of the Son of God, to a mature man, to the measure of the stature which belongs to the fulness of Christ.

Here we see that the Lord gave His church a diversity of ministries for equipping the church. These ministries are called to work as a team, which was demonstrated beautifully in the first century. After the first century this team concept eroded, and with it the spiritual power and authority of the church.

It is noteworthy that this is the only place in the New Testament where the ministry of the pastor is mentioned. Yet, until recently it has almost completely dominated the ministry of the church. My point in bringing up this issue is not to detract from the pastor's ministry. I believe it is intended to be much more

129

than it typically is today. Even so, pastors will never become what they are supposed to be until they take their place as a part of the team of ministries that the Lord gave for the equipping of His church.

Many pastors are trying to be all of the equipping ministries simultaneously for their church. This not only dilutes their ability to do what they are called and anointed to do, but it also cuts off the development and functioning of those who are supposed to be operating in the other ministries. This greatly reduces the effectiveness of the entire church. We are not far from the time when no ministry will be able to survive which is not a part of a team.

In the last three decades there has been a growing chorus of church leaders who have begun to recognize the need for all of the equipping ministries listed above, Many are now recognizing them. Many have carried it a bit too far and started awarding titles a little too cheaply, but even so, the advancing church is moving toward the recognition and implementation of all of the equipping ministries given to the church. We simply cannot become the church we are called to be without them.

Many people believe that there are no longer apostles and prophets because we do not need them after the Scriptures were written. However, the Scriptures clearly refutes this, as our text states that all of the ministries are given to the church *"until* **we all attain to the unity of the faith, the knowledge of the Son of God...the measure of the stature which belongs to the fulness of Christ."** Has any church in all of history attained to this yet? I have not witnessed or even heard of one that we might consider even close to this, so we obviously still need all of these ministries.

This is now old news to most who are a part of the advancing church, but one crucial question that we should ask: Are those churches that recognize and receive all of these equipping ministries getting closer to the goal? Recognizing and receiving these ministries is a start, but is the equipping actually taking place? It is my opinion that this is rarely happening even in those churches that recognize these ministries. In them there may be a few more people who are recognized in ministry, and a few more equipped, but overall we are falling far short of what we could call an effective equipping ministry in the church.

This is truly one of the important issues of our time, and must be addressed if we are going to fulfill our mandate as the church. We will therefore dwell on this issue for the next few chapters in order to seek practical answers. However, before going on, please allow me to offer what I think is the most basic issue that we have to understand in order to properly address this fundamental problem in the church.

The first thing these ministries are given to do is to help us come to the knowledge of the Son of God. This was the true apostolic mandate, and is the foundation of all true equipping and ministry. To grow in our ministry we are not just growing up into a job, but into a person—Jesus Christ. All true New Testament ministry is found in Him, and imparted to us as we behold His glory.

Ministry is simply the fruit of growing in Christlikeness. We do this by beholding Him. Therefore, the central message of all true New Testament ministries will be Christ Himself, not just a doctrine, and not just issues such as church government and organization. Our effectiveness in true ministry will therefore be only to the degree that we are beholding Him, and are captured ourselves by the centrality of Christ Himself in everything. In the coming chapters we will examine this a little more thoroughly.

CHAPTER TWENTY-EIGHT

Defining Our Calling

Our goal for this study is to methodically sink our roots deeper into sound biblical truth, as well as the important spiritual issues of our times, so we can walk in our ultimate purpose. For this reason we want to delve a little deeper into the text that we began to study in the last chapter, Ephesians 4:11-13:

> **And He gave some as apostles, and some as prophets, and some as evangelists, and some as pastors and teachers,**
>
> **for the equipping of the saints for the work of service, to the building up of the body of Christ;**
>
> **until we all attain to the unity of the faith, and of the knowledge of the Son of God, to a mature man, to the measure of the stature which belongs to the fulness of Christ.**

Here we have the ministries listed that are to equip the church for its ultimate purpose, which should be attaining **"the measure of the stature which belongs to the fulness of Christ."** This must be our ultimate goal, and the focus that motivates all that we do in ministry. Anything that deviates from this simplicity of purpose will sidetrack us from our calling. Growing up into the Lord Jesus Himself, knowing Him and abiding in Him, is our goal.

Now we will give a brief description of each of these ministries that are given to the church for this purpose beginning with the first listed—the apostle. We are told in Hebrews 3:1, **"Therefore, holy brethren, partakers of a heavenly calling, consider Jesus, the Apostle and High Priest of our confession."** Jesus is the Apostle, just as He was the Prophet, Evangelist, Shepherd, and Teacher. When we grow in ministry, we are in fact growing up into that aspect of Him.

The apostolic ministry itself is basically a composite of all of the other ministries. For example, we can see that the primary apostles in Scripture, Peter, John, and Paul, were all great teachers and were certainly pastoral, all prophesied, and did the work of an evangelist. However, this does not mean that someone who tends to be all of these things is an apostle. Why? Because the apostolic ministry is more than just a function—it is a commission.

Any believer, even one who really is not called to one of the equipping ministries, can at times be used to teach, shepherd others, prophesy, or lead people to the Lord. To be one of these equipping ministries requires a commission. The apostolic ministry requires a personal commission from the Lord Himself. This does not just come in an impression or prophetic word. As the apostle Paul mentions in Acts 9:27, the first thing he states to verify his apostolic ministry is having **"seen the Lord."** Obviously he was talking of more than just a dream or vision here.

Why must an apostle see the Lord? The apostles are the "master-builders" of the temple of the Lord, which is the church. Like Moses, the first in Scripture to build a habitation of the Lord, who had to go up on the mountain to see a model of the tabernacle before he could build it, the apostle must have a clear vision of what he is to build. The model of the church is Jesus Himself. There is something about beholding the glory and majesty of who He is that imparts an understanding, a focus, and a resolve that is essential for true apostolic authority.

The ultimate apostolic burden can be summed up in Galatians 4:19: **"My children, with whom I am again in labor until Christ is formed in you..."**

Many popular definitions of apostolic ministry focus on what are really more administrative gifts than apostolic. The ability to recruit churches into an organization, or teach on church government, may be done by people who do not even have one of the equipping ministries listed here. A good multi-level marketer can do that. The true apostolic anointing compels the church to draw near to the Lord, to behold Him, and to be conformed to His image, not just grow a system.

Besides having the authority to build, there are also other issues related to the apostolic ministry such as tearing down, addressing error, heresy, and apostasy. One of the reasons why there is so much confusion and disputes about doctrine today is because of the lack of true apostolic authority in the church. When this ministry is fully restored to the church it will have an authority to confront the great issues with the wisdom from above that will be above reproach or dispute. Such authority does not come from a title, but a substance and anointing that human wisdom cannot refute.

In Proverbs 24:3-4 we are told that **"By wisdom a house is built, and by understanding it is established; and by knowledge the rooms are filled..."** It is wisdom that actually builds the house. Knowledge will draw crowds, and we have often tried to draw crowds before building the house. When this is done we do not have real churches, but crowds that gather. This will change when the true apostolic ministry is restored. They will primarily come with wisdom, not just knowledge. Therefore they may not draw as many people, but they will build something that the Lord Himself will want to inhabit.

There was also a fundamental apostolic characteristic of being boldly pioneering in nature that is seen in all of the biblical apostles. This is a drive to go further, higher, and deeper, which compels others to do the same. There is nothing in this world more contagious than one who is getting closer to the Lord, and this is the pre-eminent drive of apostolic ministry. This could be classified simply as leadership. However, this is a leadership that does not just dictate direction, but in fact leads.

When true apostolic ministry appears, the church will be drawn into more of all that she is called to walk in. This is an intangible which can only come by the special anointing that is reserved for those who are of the substance that can be so endorsed. However, because this ministry is the composite of all of the other equipping ministries as well, it will also be utterly practical in teaching, counseling, imparting vision and direction, as well as in reaching the lost.

There is no question that the church is in need of apostolic leadership at this time. However, we cannot settle for cheap substitutes. If we want the real thing we must be willing to wait for it. Apostles are not made overnight. Even the apostle Paul was called as an apostle many years before he was commissioned to this ministry. Then he was a very immature apostle until he grew and gained experience. One of the primary reasons for the superficiality of the church today is the superficiality of those we have been willing to follow.

Just as the Lord commended the Ephesian church in the book of Revelation for putting to the test those who called themselves apostles and were not, this is one issue that is too important to overlook. We can err in either missing the time of our visitation by not recognizing those who have an authentic apostolic ministry, or we can err by receiving too easily those who do not really have the ministry even though they claim to. Remember, there is a ditch on either side of the path of life, but when you are on the path, you will know it because of the life that is flowing.

CHAPTER TWENTY-NINE

The Prophets

In the last chapter we took a rather cursory look at the apostolic ministry to begin our study of the equipping ministries listed in Ephesians 4. In this chapter we will continue with the next ministry that is mentioned—the prophets. Of course, the very best that we can do in such a short format as this book is necessarily superficial, and we are therefore just trying to touch on some of the important highlights of each of these ministries.

As we discussed in relation to the apostle, we may perform all of the functions of the apostolic ministry at times but that does not make us an apostle. Likewise, one may be used to prophesy but that does not necessarily make them a prophet. In fact, Paul wrote that **"you can all prophesy" (I Corinthians 14:31).** We also read in Acts 2:17:

> **"And it shall be in the last days,' God says, "That I will pour forth of My Spirit upon all mankind; and your sons and your daughters shall prophesy, and your young men shall see visions, and your old men shall dream dreams."**

Here we see that when the Lord pours out His Spirit everyone prophesies—young and old, male and female. So just having prophetic revelation does not make one a prophet.

So what does make one a prophet? Again, these ministries listed in Ephesians 4 are offices that one must be commissioned to. There is a difference between being called and being commissioned to that ministry, just as Paul was called to be an apostle many years before he was commissioned to it.

So how does one know when they are commissioned? If you have to ask if you have been commissioned, it has not happened yet. When you are commissioned by the Lord to a ministry you will know it. There are many different ways that He commissions His ministries in Scripture, but all of them leave no doubt that it has been done. So, what does the commission do for us that changes things from when we were not yet commissioned?

The time between the calling and the commissioning is the time of preparation for our ministry. We may do all of the things that a commissioned ministry would do, and it should be a time when we are especially growing in the spiritual gifts that we have been given in preparation for our ministry. However, when the commission comes, there will be an increased authority and anointing that comes with it. The commission is a special endorsement from the Lord Himself that He recognizes and backs up our ministry.

In the world we recognize someone's position and submit to their authority because of that position. If you are in the army and one has on the bars of a captain, they will be related to according to their rank. Some will be compelled to submit to their authority, and those who are higher in rank will expect the lower ranking officer to submit to them. This is regardless of who is the more intelligent, the more resourceful, or who is the greater leader. It is not supposed to be the same thing in the church. We seek to be led by the Holy Spirit, and therefore recognize the anointing and commissions that are on someone's life. Only the truly spiritual can understand this, much less do it. Even so, it is something that we must mature into if the church is going to be what it is called to be in the last days.

So what do prophets do that distinguishes them from the other equipping ministries? Prophets are called to hear from the Lord on a strategic level. This has nothing to do with teaching, writing, or establishing doctrine, but rather the revealing of the will of the Lord in certain matters. This can be for individuals, churches, the universal church, or even for governments, businesses, or other entities to which the Lord wants to speak.

The ways in which prophets receive revelation from the Lord are as diverse in Scripture as the prophets themselves. It can come by an impression, dreams, visions, the word of the Lord, angelic visitations, or being caught up in the Spirit, and even to stand before the Lord. This makes the prophet's ministry exceptionally exciting. The Lord seems intent on speaking in ways that not only convey the message, but reveal His heart in a matter, and His ways. For this reason very often the way in which the revelation comes, and to which particular prophet it comes, can be a significant part of the message.

We are also told that we **"prophesy in part."** This means that regardless of how spectacularly our revelation came, it is but a part of the whole picture. Therefore, if we are to have the complete picture we must learn to put our part together with what others are seeing. That is why this ministry is almost always referred to in the plural.

In Matthew 23:34 the Lord said, **"Therefore, behold, I am sending you prophets and wise men and scribes..."** For the sake of clarity we need to make a distinction between these three specific emissaries that the Lord promises to send us: 1) **"prophets,"** 2) **"wise men,"** and 3) **"scribes."** Prophets are sent with words and revelation from the Lord. Wise men have the wisdom that builds in relation to the apostolic ministry. Scribes are writers. Each of these have a different function and authority.

We had a good example of spiritual authority recently when the stock markets were tumbling. I watched with interest as the President tried to reassure and stabilize them with a speech about how good the economy was doing. The markets dropped even more. Then Alan Greenspan, the head of the Federal Reserve, basically said the same things the next day and there was an immediate positive effect. Certainly the President has more authority by his position than the head of the Federal Reserve, but he does not have more authority in relation to the economy. Both were really trying to address a spiritual issue—fear. Alan Greenspan has built a long record of credibility that the business community respects. He is a wise man in this area. The President does not have that kind of record yet in relation to the economy, so even though he has a much higher position, Greenspan has more spiritual authority than the President does in some areas.

Now, suppose someone has established a credibility that he really has heard from God so that his message was believed to have actually come straight from God? That would be a different kind of authority than the wise man has by his wisdom. The prophetic authority that comes from having a track record of hearing accurately from God does certainly stand out over just having wisdom. This kind of spiritual authority does not happen overnight, unless it comes with spectacular, supernatural manifestations. We see prophets in Scripture gaining authority both ways. With some, the Lord endorsed them with great supernatural power. With others, they grew in stature because none of their words "fell to the ground." Usually prophetic authority is a combination of both.

However, we do need to distinguish prophetic authority from the authority of the **"wise men."** The prophets are sent to deliver messages from God, not just have good advice. Just as we discussed with the apostolic ministry, we do not want to settle for cheap substitutes.

Acts 2:17 states that **"in the last days"** when the Lord pours out His Spirit, it results in prophecy, dreams, visions, and even **"… wonders in the sky above, and signs on the earth beneath…"** We are living in a time of great increase in the prophetic gifts and manifestations. Just as Acts 2:17 states, it is happening to the old and young, men and women, which includes *everyone*. So it is even more important in these times when the Spirit is being poured out that we learn to distinguish the office of the prophet from those who just receive prophetic revelation, which will ultimately be everyone.

The office of the prophet comes by a commission from God, not just the level or even the importance of revelation received.

As we are told concerning this, and all of the other ministries listed in Ephesians 4, one of its primary functions is to equip the saints. This means that a prophet should not only be hearing from God on a prophetic level, but he should be equipping those that he ministers to so that they know the voice of the Lord and hear from Him.

There is far more to this ministry than we can give attention to in this book, but as this has been something of a specialty of our ministry at MorningStar, we do have books and teaching tapes available on the prophetic ministry and gifts that are available in many Christian bookstores, or can be ordered by calling our ministry at 1-800-542-0278, or through our website www.morningstarministries.org.

CHAPTER THIRTY

The Evangelist

Continuing our study of the equipping ministries listed in Ephesians 4:11, we will take a brief look at the ministry of the evangelist in this chapter.

In the New Testament we have over twenty people who are referred to as apostles, only a few who are referred to as prophets, and only one who is called an evangelist—Philip (see Acts 21:8). Timothy was instructed by Paul to **"do the work of an evangelist" (II Timothy 4:5),** but was never called an evangelist. It is interesting that next to the pastor, we do not have any real examples in Scripture of the New Testament evangelist. The evangelist is the second most recognized of the ministries today even though in the early church this was obviously not the case.

The Greek word that is translated in these verses **"evangelist,"** is *euaggelistes,* which literally means "a good messenger," or "messenger of good," or "good news." From the beginning it was used in reference to those who preached the gospel.

In this sense, all of the apostles were also evangelists. However, this was but one of their many duties. There were those whose entire ministry was to preach the gospel bringing the opportunity of salvation to the unsaved. Philip, who was appointed with Stephen as one of the seven deacons in Jerusalem, is the only example that we are given of this ministry in the New Testament. From Acts 8 we see that he operated alone, and his ministry was limited to bringing the people to salvation. He needed the apostles to come behind him to establish those who embraced salvation into a church. Even though Philip demonstrated remarkable signs and wonders so as to stir the entire city, in this case it was the apostles who prayed for the people to receive the baptism in the Holy Spirit.

We then see Philip right at the height of this revival of an entire city being led away to preach the gospel to just one man in the desert. That would require remarkable sensitivity and obedience to the Spirit, as well as submission to the ministry that God had given to the others, i.e. the apostles. Philip was obviously not possessive of his work, and recognized his own limitations.

Today the Southern Baptists seem to recognize this ministry, and have learned to utilize it possibly better than any other segment of the body of Christ. When one demonstrates this anointing among the Baptists, they put a very high value on it, and try to promote those with this gift by providing support for crusades and other outreaches. The bigger ones, such as Billy Graham, try to enlist the rest of the body of Christ in their efforts to reach a city. It is therefore not surprising that some of the most effective evangelists of our times have come through the ranks of the Southern Baptists.

Because Paul instructed Timothy to **"do the work of an evangelist,"** many have construed this to mean that all are called to do this. Certainly we should always be ready to share the hope that is within us. It is noteworthy that studies have shown that more than 95 percent of those who come to salvation do so through the witness of a friend or relative. This means that less than 5 percent come through crusades, Christian television, tracts, and all other forms of witnessing combined. This brings us to an important point concerning the ministry of the evangelist—their primary responsibility is to equip the saints to do the work of the ministry as is the case with all of these ministries listed in Ephesians 4:11.

It is the special function of the evangelist to impart a love for the lost world, and a passion for reaching the lost. The fact that 95 percent of those who come to Christ come through the witnessing of individual believers, is in fact the way it should be, and should be considered a testimony of the success of the evangelists in the church today.

However, though we may have the ratio right, the numbers of new conversions are growing dramatically almost everywhere on earth except in the United States and Western Europe. These are the primary places where the church has been experiencing a meltdown of devotion to biblical morality, integrity, and sound doctrine. Because the majority of evangelism is relational, one of the most crucial elements to effective evangelism is an encouraged church. When immorality, impurity, and a departure from sound doctrine begins to creep in, the light begins to dim, and the witness of the church stops.

In II Corinthians 13:5 we are exhorted to **"Test yourselves to see if you are in the faith; examine yourselves!"** One way that we can do this is by how we are reaching the lost. Regardless of how mature we have become, we are not walking in the light unless it is setting free those who are in darkness. This is a basic characteristic of everyone who walked in the light in both Scripture and in history. We can make all manner of excuses for not reaching the lost and saving souls, but we should be examining ourselves to find out what is wrong.

One of the things that we have started doing at the end of most of our services is giving a brief but direct call to salvation regardless of what the message was about. The result has been that in almost every service where we have done this, there has been at least one new convert, and often many more. We started this because studies have shown that less than 25 percent of those in Pentecostal and Charismatic churches have been baptized in the Holy Spirit. Others have found that there can be a majority of people in conservative evangelical churches who have never had a born again experience.

One friend of mine gave a brief salvation message at the end of a service in one of the most highly respected evangelical churches in the country. He only expected a handful to come forward, and was shocked when hundreds poured out of their seats to be born again. The pastor was so humiliated that he accused the evangelist of heaping condemnation on the people, but that was not the case. These people were in this church because they believed in it, and wanted it. Even though some of them had faithfully attended this church for years, no one had told them how to be born again, or led them through a salvation prayer.

Of course we can point to many churches that are so focused on the salvation message that they fail to feed and help mature the sheep who have already come to salvation. However, there seems to have been an overreaction to this. Many presume that those who are attending their church have been born again when they have not. Even so, to empathize a bit with the pastor noted above, the church meetings should be for believers, not unbelievers. If we equipped our people properly to do the work of evangelism, every home of our members would be a lighthouse for salvation, as well as every home group and prayer meeting. They would be leading people to salvation at work, while shopping, at the Lions Club, etc.

Like all of these ministries, we can only touch on them very briefly here. My goal is to stir up the gifts that have been dormant. If just one in each congregation is stirred up, many more will catch on. If this has stirred or convicted you in any way please continue pursuing the Lord in this. What could be more important in your life than leading even a single soul to salvation?

CHAPTER THIRTY-ONE

The Pastor

In our study of the equipping ministries listed in Ephesians 4:11, we now come to the ministry of the pastor. We discussed how there are more than twenty people in the New Testament who are referred to as apostles, only a couple who are referred to as prophets, and only one who is called an evangelist—Philip. We do not have a single person in the New Testament who is called a pastor. This verse, Ephesians 4:11, is the only place in the New Testament where this ministry is even mentioned. This leads us to a very important question—how did this ministry which is only listed one time, with no definition, and not a single New Testament example of it given, come to so dominate the ministry of the church?

First, we should not immediately conclude that this is wrong, or at least entirely wrong. Although we do not have an explicit example of this ministry in the New Testament, we have an implicit one in the Lord Himself, just as we do all of the ministries. Leading and guiding the flock is basic to how the Lord shepherds His flock, which He does primarily through those to which He has given this ministry.

The Greek word translated **"pastor"** here is *poimen,* which is defined as "a shepherd, one who tends herds or flocks," not merely one who feeds them. Tending speaks of protecting them from predators, keeping them healthy, examining their pastures for any noxious vegetation, as well as providing them with pure water to drink. All of these are likewise the responsibility of this ministry in the church.

It should be noted that the elders were also instructed to shepherd the flock of God, as we see in Acts 20:28-30:

> **Be on guard for yourselves and for all the flock, among which the Holy Spirit has made you overseers, to shepherd the church of God which He purchased with His own blood.**
>
> **"I know that after my departure savage wolves will come in among you, not sparing the flock;**
>
> **and from among your own selves men will arise, speaking perverse things, to draw away the disciples after them.**

It should also be noted that this instruction is given to the "elders," plural. Not once in the New Testament do we see just one person being called "the pastor." It seems obvious that this was always intended to be a team effort. This should not be construed as meaning that elders or pastors are supposed to be co-equal in authority or leadership. In fact, the New Testament pattern for leadership is that one normally leads the team, such as Peter and James did in Jerusalem. Even so, there is nonetheless a team of elders and apostles in every case. No one man can be everything to the flock of God that shepherding requires. Those who are under a single person who tries to be all things to all people are inevitably poorly cared for sheep.

Nevertheless, pastors are constantly bombarded by such foolish notions as "My life (or my children, my ministry...) would not be in such bad shape if we had a better pastor!" The expectations put on pastors are not only unrealistic, but sadistic and cruel. Even the greatest pastor is not God, and no pastor is here to take God's place in our life.

Even so, the Lord gave us the metaphor of sheep and shepherds because the characteristics of sheep to people, and people who are anointed as shepherds, which provide guidance to His people, are similar. A good shepherd, like the Lord, is not a hireling who is just doing a job, but is one who so loves the sheep that he will lay down his own life for them. A good shepherd will also want the sheep to always have the best pastures, the best water, and will always be vigilant to insure their protection.

One of the most basic requirements for a healthy flock is crossbreeding with other flocks. Any flock that does not cross-breed with other flocks will get weaker with each succeeding generation. The same is true in the church. If we do not have fellowship and interchange with other believers and churches that are different from ours, we will get continually weaker instead of stronger. Therefore, shepherds that are possessive or fearful of other churches and ministries will probably do more long term damage to their own flock than any problems that they could have encountered by interchange with others.

We also see in the New Testament that apostles called themselves elders. However, this should not be construed that they considered themselves elders of the local churches, but they were elders with a much more broad sphere of authority in the church. There are spheres of authority and levels of authority in the church that we need to recognize and stay within, from both directions.

What I mean by staying within our spheres of authority from both directions is that even if you are an apostle over an entire movement, and therefore have the shepherding responsibilities over it, you should not interfere with what you have delegated to your elders or other leaders on the local level unless it is by their request. That is why such a large number of the Epistles in the New Testament were actually letters written in response to letters, with specific questions from the churches.

Also, because I Corinthians 11:3 states that **"...Christ is the head of every man..."** even if I was an apostle there are things in a believer's life that are his business and I would not interfere with. I would not interfere in his marriage or family unless there were serious transgressions that were affecting others in the church, etc. However, in that case I would not hesitate to use my authority for the sake of the man, his family, and the church. Even so, as much as possible, all spiritual authority should be exercised with the utmost respect for each other and the delegated spheres of authority.

True authority releases others into greater authority by giving them more responsibility. True spiritual authority is always trying to bring those under authority to the place of maturity and wisdom so that they no longer need our authority, but have their own. Even the King of kings said that it was expedient for His disciples that He go away so that the Spirit could come directly to them. This was the best way for them to grow up into Him. There is a point at which spiritual shepherding breaks down the metaphor of sheep and shepherds, which is why we should be seeking to turn all of our sheep into shepherds. That is why this is an "equipping" ministry.

As we also discussed in relation to the other equipping ministries, they are all called to equip the saints who are to do the work of the ministry. A prophet's job is not to just prophesy, but to equip the saints to know the Lord's voice for themselves, and to be used by Him to prophesy. An evangelist does not just preach the gospel himself, but he equips the church to preach the gospel and to have a burden for the lost. The same is true of the pastor ministry—it is given to help all believers to embrace the shepherding heart of the Lord at least to some degree. We should all be able to discern when a brother or sister is in trouble, and to know how to help them.

Another basic element that we must keep in mind in relation to the pastor is that the most basic foundation of this ministry is not love for the sheep, but rather love for the Lord. We must love the sheep of course, but we will love them wrongly if we do not love the Lord even more. That is what the Lord tried to impart to Peter in John 21:15-17:

> **So when they had finished breakfast, Jesus said to Simon Peter, "Simon, son of John, do you love Me more than these?" He said to Him, "Yes, Lord; You know that I love You." He said to him, "Tend My lambs."**

He said to him again a second time, "Simon, son of John, do you love Me?" He said to Him, "Yes, Lord; You know that I love You." He said to him, "Shepherd My sheep."

He said to him the third time, "Simon, son of John, do you love Me?" Peter was grieved because He said to him the third time, "Do you love Me?" And he said to Him," Lord, You know all things; You know that I love You. "Jesus said to him," Tend My sheep.

Here we see Peter being told that if he loved the Lord he would: 1) tend His lambs, 2) shepherd His sheep, and 3) tend His sheep. It begins with the young ones and emphasizes both shepherding and tending the sheep. All of this we too will do if we love Him.

CHAPTER   THIRTY-TWO

The Teacher

The teacher is the last of the five equipping ministries listed in Ephesians 4:11, but it is foundational to all of the other ministries. To equip others requires teaching as well as training and impartation. However, the teaching ministry is one that focuses on imparting the knowledge of God's ways, especially as revealed through the Scriptures, by the Spirit.

As with the ministry of the pastor, we do not have a New Testament example of one who was exclusively a teacher, though we have in Acts 13:1 a list of five men who were **"prophets and teachers."** Obviously some of these were prophets and some were teachers, but we do not know which ones were which. Even so, this brings us to an important point. It was when the prophets and teachers were worshiping the Lord together that apostolic ministries were birthed. It is the special joining of these two ministries today that is especially needed in order to release true apostolic ministry again.

Teachers will tend to be more practical, while prophets tend to deal more in the area of vision—where we need to be rather than how to get there. When these two ministries work together they will almost always make a dynamic and powerful team that can accomplish great things. When they operate separately both cannot only be ineffective, but destructive. Teachers without the influence of prophets will often be so practical that the people may have sound doctrine, but lack the fire and vision that forward progress always requires. Prophets without the influence of teachers can have everybody fired up but not knowing what to do.

All of these equipping ministries are designed to function as a team, and as a team it will be the most dynamic and powerful leadership force on earth. As individuals they can all accomplish some things, but far less than what can be done when together. We should also note that when acting as a team it does not mean that they need to be together all of the time. In the New Testament we see how some would go to a city and plant a church or minister to one, and then another group would come later to follow up on the work. As Paul related, in this way some planted, another group watered, but God gave the increase (see I Corinthians 3:6-7).

Now back to the specific function of the teacher. The heart and soul of the teaching ministry is a love for the truth. This love will always compel one to search the Scriptures, which is the foundation of all truth. I Corinthians 2:10 reveals an important point about the teacher: **"For to us God revealed them through the Spirit; for the Spirit searches all things, even the depths of God."** It is the Spirit that compels us to search the depths of God, and it is also the Spirit that must reveal them. For this reason the teacher must be as sensitive to the Spirit as any other ministry. Hermeneutics and other systems of study can be helpful guidelines, but if we begin to rely on them in place of the Spirit we will be deceived. The Spiritual truth of God cannot be found out by a science, but must be revealed by the Spirit of truth. This is one of the primary reasons for which the Spirit was given, to lead us into all truth.

For the teacher to equip the saints, more is required than just imparting knowledge. The primary job of the teacher is to impart a love for the truth. This will compel the saints to dig their own wells, which is essential for a true faith. No one will get into the kingdom because they know someone who knows the Lord—we all must know Him for ourselves. We all must know the truth for ourselves. The true teacher imparts such a love of the knowledge of God's ways that those who hear are drawn to the Word themselves.

CHAPTER THIRTY-THREE

The Purpose of Ministry

For the last few chapters we have briefly discussed the functions of the five equipping ministries listed in Ephesians 4:11. Now we will proceed to discuss their purpose in a little more depth, which we have repeatedly stated as being **"for the equipping of the saints for the work of service, to the building up of the body of Christ" (Ephesians 4:12).** So what does it mean to "equip" the saints?

We often think of equipping as teaching but it is more than that. Training is more than just teaching, but equipping is even more than that. For example, when one is enlisted in the army, a soldier is taught about weapons and basic battlefield strategy in classrooms. Then they are taken into the field and trained to do what they have been taught from the textbooks. However, they are not equipped until they are given their weapons. The same is true in the church. In II Corinthians 10:3-4 we are told:

> **For though we walk in the flesh, we do not war according to the flesh,**
>
> **for the weapons of our warfare are not of the flesh, but divinely powerful for the destruction of fortresses.**

We might ask one question here that will highlight the degree of effectiveness of the present ministry of the church— how many Christians do you know who are equipped with divinely powerful weapons and are tearing down evil strongholds? Every Christian should have notches on their belts from all of the evil strongholds they have torn down! Why don't we?

Everywhere from school curriculums, to Hollywood, to the media, powerful evil strongholds are growing in number and in power, turning people away from the truth and toward evil. Where are the divinely powerful weapons that can tear them down? What are they? Picketing and demonstrating against evil has accomplished little more than wearing out the saints. There has to be more power to confront and bring down evil than what we are now experiencing.

Truth spoken under the anointing is our most powerful weapon. This weapon can only be used from the strong fortress of a heart that is in unity with the truth. This is our first and most important devotion, to build up the body of Christ so that it is an impregnable fortress for truth and righteousness. Then we can be trusted with the prophetic unction to expose the darkness and call people back to the standards of righteousness that are already written throughout the creation. As we are told in Romans 1:20:

For since the creation of the world His invisible attributes, His eternal power and divine nature, have been clearly seen, being understood through what has been made, so that they are without excuse.

The law of God's righteous ways are not only written throughout the creation, but they are also a witness in the conscience of every human being. Our consciences can become **"seared" (I Timothy 4:2)**, insensitive, by continually doing what we know to be evil, but the witness of God's ways is already sown through the creation, including mankind. Our goal is to return to the solid rock of living by the truth that is more fundamental and obvious than any other, and awakening this in others so that they cast off the chains of darkness to live by the Light.

One of the most powerful examples of the power of the anointing to change the world is in the life of John Calvin.

Regardless of what we may think of his theology, he is one of the most remarkable men to have ever lived. What Calvin accomplished in Geneva would be the equivalent of having a pastor of a church dictate policy throughout a world-class city simply by the power of his preaching. Without holding a political office, and without even being a Swiss citizen, he ruled Geneva more thoroughly from his pulpit than any potentate by simply preaching the Word. A sermon from him could unravel the most powerful evil stronghold over the people of that city, and in fact spread to many other countries, as well as other centuries. No law or code was passed without his approval in Geneva, and the force of his opinion on a matter carried more weight than all other city officials combined. How? He spoke by the anointing with perfect clarity into the great issues of his time. No one could gainsay his wisdom or the anointing, which was backed up by a life that was consistent and true.

Such influence cannot be explained by the force of mere human personality or charisma. It is a spiritual authority the Lord does not give cheaply. Even so, it should be the goal of every believer to have the light within them have more influence over their environment than any power or philosophy from hell ever could. Christians in the first century had this kind of power, and we should not settle for anything less in our own.

To do this we must go to a new level of teaching, training, and equipping of believers. Like a new army recruit, a believer must be first taught the standards of God's righteousness and His ways, the schemes of the enemy, and how we are to live. They must then be trained, just as soldiers are taken to the field to practice, to learn to shoot and take care of their weapons until they are effective with them. The Christian life should be even more challenging, requiring more devotion and training than any special forces.

True Christianity is the most challenging life we can have, but also the most fulfilling. It is the ultimate adventure. It is far more than attending a couple of boring meetings a week. The reality of true Christianity must be recovered, and the power of the truth we have been entrusted with restored.

We can count on this happening before the end of this age, but the church must become an army of disciplined spiritual soldiers who are effective with the gifts and ministries entrusted to them, and become the most effective, glorious people who have ever been released on the earth. This will happen when the ministry of the church becomes the team that it is called to be, and starts to do its basic work—equipping the saints to do what they are called to do.

PART V

A More Solid Foundation

A Study of Ephesians Chapter 4:14-32

CHAPTER THIRTY-FOUR

Stability and Discernment

In Part Five, we will be studying the last verses of Ephesians 4. They represent an important teaching for developing a strong foundation upon which every Christian life should be built. In this chapter we continue our study with Ephesians 4:14:

As a result, we are no longer to be children, tossed here and there by waves, and carried about by every wind of doctrine, by the trickery of men, by craftiness in deceitful scheming;

This mature condition is the result of believers being equipped by the ministries listed in verse 11 of Ephesians 4. If we look at this in reverse, we could say that the reason for immaturity and instability of Christians is their tendency to sit under only one ministry, which is the case for a good portion of the body of Christ. In fact, one definition of a cult is a group that listens to only one prophet or teacher.

To be effectively established and prepared for our purpose, we need an impartation from each of the equipping ministries, not just one, or even two. A secular education requires many different teachers for many different subjects, which are all needed to prepare one for a vocation in the modern world. Christianity was the first religion to emphasize education and training in righteousness for all who were committed to the faith. The true Christian life is one of progression in understanding, demeanor, and in the power to do good. That is why we are told in Proverbs 4:18, "**...the path of the righteous is like the light of dawn, that shines brighter and brighter until the full day.**"

As this verse states, if the light in which we walk is not getting brighter and brighter, then we have somehow departed from the path. One of the reasons why Christians are called disciples is because disciples are students who are learning. The true Christian life is a life of continual enlightenment and of being changed into the image of the God we worship.

For this reason we need teachers to help ground us in solid biblical truth, and to impart a love for the truth so that we will search the Scriptures ourselves. We need pastors to help guide us in the ways of the Lord, and to equip us to love and help watch over one another. We need evangelists to impart God's love to us for the lost, as well as to equip us to release the light that we have been given to lead others out of darkness and into the light of the Lord. We need prophets for strategic guidance, and to teach us how to know the voice of the Lord. We need apostles to help take all of the different parts of the body and fit them together into a functioning whole body. From this we see how all of these are needed for a balanced, healthy, Christian life.

Let us break this verse down a little further. As a result of being properly equipped: 1) we will no longer be children, 2) we will not be tossed about by waves, 3) we will not be "**carried about by every wind of doctrine,**" 4) we will not succumb to the "**trickery of men**" and, 5) we will not be misled by "**craftiness in deceitful scheming.**"

It does not take long to realize that the church has not done well in these basics since the first century. This is the result of us not having received from all of the equipping ministries that are given to the church for these purposes. New Testament ministry is called to be a team, and any team that is lacking members will be weakened. Most churches are actually missing four-fifths of their ministry because they only basically receive from one ministry—the pastor. How good would any team be that was missing 80 percent of its players? This is what has happened to the ministry of the church.

Now let us take a brief, but more in-depth look at these five strengths that are the result of receiving the ministry of all five of those given for the equipping of believers.

1) <u>We are to no longer be children.</u> This means that we should grow up. It is interesting that the author of the most meaty book in the New Testament that is not prophetic, the book of Hebrews, teaches on such subjects as the Melchizedek priesthood, and laments that he can only share with his readers, milk and not solid food! Is there even a church in the world today that understands the book of Hebrews, which the writer calls baby food? The ones that I have found with even a hint of the knowledge which should be basic to every Christian, are still lacking in the practical training necessary so that their people are actually walking in that knowledge.

The goal is that we are all equipped to be teachers and to prophesy. We should all be able to heal the sick, cast out demons, and have the wisdom of Solomon because One greater than Solomon lives inside of us! Where is the depth, the maturing in godliness, and the knowledge of the ways of God? We will not have it until all of the equipping ministries are in their place and functioning.

2) <u>We are not to be tossed about by waves.</u> Moves of the Holy Spirit are usually referred to as waves. Could this mean that the mature will not be tossed about by the waves of the Holy Spirit? Yes. The Holy Spirit is doing many wonderful things in the earth at this present time, but if we tried to be a part of every one of them, we would be like a cork tossed by the waves of the sea. We must be discerning as to what the Lord is doing in us, and be happy for what He is doing in others, but not feel we need to chase everything that is going on in the body of Christ. This kind of maturity and discernment comes from being properly grounded in our relationship to the Lord so that we know what He is doing in us and are secure in it.

3) <u>We will not be "carried about by every wind of doctrine."</u> It is interesting that there is no mention here of these being false doctrines. Like trying to follow every wave of the Holy Spirit,

we can actually be carried about and become superficial in our faith by trying to chase every new teaching that is coming out in the body of Christ. If we are going to be stable and go on to maturity we must recognize what the Lord is trying to teach us personally, and sink our roots deeply in those things and not chase all of the other things that He is teaching others.

4) <u>We will not be fooled by the "trickery of men."</u> Paul wrote in II Corinthians 11:20, **"For you bear with anyone if he enslaves you, if he devours you, if he takes advantage of you, if he exalts himself, if he hits you in the face."** It is shocking the way so many believers are prone to follow those with the nature of a spiritual bully, which is actually contrary to the nature of Christ. Again, we are in a most desperate need of discernment in the body of Christ, and it will only come when there is the balanced ministry present as in the team of ministries listed in Ephesians 4:11.

5) <u>We will not be misled by "craftiness in deceitful scheming."</u> Craftiness is the first characteristic given to the serpent, the devil. Craftiness is the tendency to try to bend the rules and get away with it. This is a characteristic of the devil and when we see it operating in someone it is a good indication that they are also involved in scheming and deception. Again, the answer to this is what was stated in the previous two verses in this text—the New Covenant ministry is designed to function as a team, and only the team that God has given for the equipping of His people will keep us on track, and lead us to the fulfillment of our purpose on the earth.

It seems that almost the entire advancing church has awakened to the need for recognizing and receiving from all of the equipping ministries the Lord gave to His church. During this awakening many seem to have gone to the other extreme and started casting these titles about somewhat prematurely, designating some as equipping ministries which do not measure up to the biblical standards of those ministries. But we ultimately can count on stability, maturity, and strength coming as the ministries are restored to the church. It is essential if we are to become the body of Christ that we are called to be.

CHAPTER THIRTY-FIVE

Speaking the Truth in Love

Now we come to one of the more amazing verses in the entire Epistle—Ephesians 4:15:

but speaking the truth in love, we are to grow up in all aspects into Him, who is the head, even Christ,

This is another one of those verses that is worthy of an entire lifetime of study by itself. In fact, if this one verse had been heeded, it is likely that literally millions of people would have avoided being destroyed in wars and persecutions by their fellow Christians during the church age. If this one verse were heeded there would be no divisions within the body of Christ today.

The Lord Jesus is the Truth and anyone who really loves Him, loves truth. We must be committed to sound, biblical truth as a basis for our lives. Even so, we will still be deceived if our truth is not balanced by love.

Truth without love has been a diabolical weapon in the hands of the enemy, which is one reason why he is also called **"an angel of light" (II Corinthians 11:14).** An angel is a messenger, and light is truth, and Satan often comes to do his evil while disguising himself as an angel from God with truth.

Just because we know some truth about someone, this does not mean we should share it. This is the stumbling block that many trip over trying to be Christian journalists. We must also consider whether we are able to share the truth in love. As verse 29 of this chapter states:

Let no unwholesome word proceed from your mouth, but only such a word as is good for edification according to the need of the moment, that it may give grace to those who hear.

Every word that comes out of our mouth should be qualified by this verse. This is actually the foundation for us to grow up **"in all aspects into Him who is the head, even Christ."** Remember that He is the Word. As He also said in John 6:63, **"It is the Spirit who gives life; the flesh profits nothing; the words that I have spoken to you are spirit and are life.** Words are precious. As we are told in Proverbs 18:21, **"Death and life are in the power of the tongue, and those who love it will eat its fruit."** What are our words producing? If we are truly growing up into Him, they will edify those who hear them, producing life—His life in others.

Our next verse, Ephesians 4:16, ties all that we have been studying over the last ten chapters into one final explanation of how we will actually grow up into who we are called to be:

from whom the whole body, being fitted and held together by that which every joint supplies, according to the proper working of each individual part, causes the growth of the body for the building up of itself in love.

For a body to be fit together properly, each member must know their own gifts and ministries, as well as that of the other members. Therefore, one of the first priorities of the equipping ministries is to help believers identify their gifts and ministries. We must then teach, train, equip, and deploy them so that they are functioning in their calling. Only then can we fit them together so that they can be built up by that which every joint supplies.

These parts are then fitted and **"held together by that which every *joint* supplies."** As with our natural body, joints are formed between different parts, not between those that are alike. Your hand is joined to a wrist, not another hand. However, if you look at the church today, for the most part all of one type, such as evangelists, will be found in one group, the teachers will tend to congregate in another, and the prophets all like to stick together, etc. Just as it takes a male and female to make a marriage, the marriage of ministries requires different parts of the body to learn to relate to each other properly.

Of course, we do not want to just fit together with any different part. You do not want a hand joined to a knee. This is why the wisdom of God's "master-builders," the apostles, is essential for a church to be structured and built up the way that the Lord intended. One of the most important gifts in the body of Christ today is the one that is able to discern which parts of the body are called to relate to other parts, and to help stimulate the interchange from which a true and lasting relationship can be built.

To begin the task of helping the church come together as it is supposed to, we need all believers to know their spiritual gifts and ministries. As stated, presently less than 10 percent of believers even know their place in the body, and far less are functioning in it. How can you know how to be joined to the rest of the body if you do not even know what part you play? Presently most churches are like large piles of living stones that are gathered but are not being built together into the temple that they are called to be. This is also why so many continue to fall away from the faith. It is easy to steal a stone that is just lying in a pile, but once it has been cemented into a wall or room, it will not so easily be taken.

Presently we must confess that the church is in a deplorable state of weakness. The failure of ministries to equip the saints so that every individual part is functioning is a primary reason for the overall ineffectiveness of the church to accomplish her mandate in this hour. How did we come to this state? We did this by letting a form of ministry evolve in the church that is a major departure from that which the Lord intended and gave us an example of in the New Testament. Even though much of the church now recognizes the ministries listed in Ephesians 4, and many are claiming the titles of these ministries, it is still difficult to find those who are only focused on equipping the saints instead of doing the ministry themselves.

As stated, only after the ministries have been identified and equipped is there a possibility of the joints of the body being formed as intended. Just as Barnabas had to go and find Paul, and then both of them get in the right place before they could be released in their ultimate callings as apostles, there are divine connections that need to be made with others that are essential for all of us to be released into our ultimate purpose.

As our verse then states, when this is accomplished it will result in **"the proper working of each individual part, (which) causes the growth of the body for the building up of itself in love."** A great deal of the present lack of love and devotion to building one another up is due to frustration—at least 90 percent of believers sense they have a calling but have not identified it, or cannot function in it with the present form of church life that is now the status quo. This breeds an insecurity that can be found at the root of many church splits as well as in other problems in the church.

No pastor's preaching or leadership is strong enough to bind people together in a way that can overcome the pressure of this deep frustration within the people who know they were called and given a purpose, but cannot fulfill it. Let the pastor have a few bad weeks in a row and see how the people begin to wander off. Not only is this pressure killing many pastors, but it is killing the people as well. We must therefore stop trying to build the church on anything but the only foundation, the Lord Jesus Himself and the way He wants to manifest Himself through His body. After we lay this foundation we must then be careful how we build upon it. The day of fire is already here that will test the quality of each man's work. Only the churches that have been built the way that the Lord intended will stand, and not only stand, but will prevail.

CHAPTER THIRTY-SIX

The Minds of the Futile

In this chapter we will begin by studying one of the more important warnings in this book, which is found in Ephesians 4:17-19:

> **This I say therefore, and affirm together with the Lord, that you walk no longer just as the Gentiles also walk, in the futility of their mind,**
>
> **being darkened in their understanding, excluded from the life of God, because of the ignorance that is in them, because of the hardness of their heart;**
>
> **and they, having become callous, have given themselves over to sensuality, for the practice of every kind of impurity with greediness.**

Let me begin by asking you a question that will illustrate just how darkened the understanding is of some of the world's supposedly most brilliant people. If you walked out on the beach one morning and found a brand new Mercedes complete with manuals, keys, and gas in the tank, what would you think of the person who tried to tell you that the ocean produced that car by millions of random accidents? You would rightly question their sanity. In fact, it would be hard to believe that the ocean could produce even a single tire! That is just how ridiculous the naturalistic philosophy is that many scientists are trying to impose on the world. As one honest physicist put it, the odds are greater for a tornado to hit a junkyard and leave behind a perfectly built Boeing 747 jetliner than for life to have evolved just the way many claim it did.

The sequential knowledge stored in the DNA of a single living cell has been estimated to be more than that contained in four entire sets of encyclopedias! The odds are actually greater that the ocean could produce such things as complex automobiles, or even jet planes, than that it could produce a single living cell.

If you add what is required for cells to join and interrelate to form even the most simple organisms, even if you gave zillions of years for this to happen, the odds would still be a decimal and so many zeros that this book could not contain them. Then if you carry it on for the millions of other random accidents that would have to happen to form the more complex organisms such as fish or birds, much less human beings, it becomes a ridiculous argument. **"The futility of their mind"** describes quite well the people who think that way.

For anyone with even a basic knowledge of the facts, and who still believes the naturalist philosophy of evolution, requires such delusion that they have without question been **"darkened in their understanding."** Yet, how is it that almost every rendition of this argument in text books, movies, or television makes the believers in God appear to be the buffoons or simpletons? Those who have been duped by the ultimate foolishness also have the audacity to project that everyone who does not agree with them is not just wrong, but foolish.

Every intellectually honest scientist cannot help but see and admit that there is a Creator responsible for the creation whose intelligence is far beyond what even the best human minds can yet fathom. To observe and consider the intricacy and wonders of the creation is a marvel that should invoke the deepest worship and adoration of the One who created it. Instead, the delusions and pride of man have used it to draw glory to the ones who "discover" it. This is certainly the way of darkened and futile minds.

To their credit there is an increasing number of scientists who readily acknowledge, "we are not alone," obviously believing there had to be a Creator. The problem that many of them then face is looking at different religions, including Christianity, and seeing how they have behaved throughout history. They cannot seem to reconcile how One who brought forth such a glorious and wonderful creation could be the same One responsible for one of those religions. This is a more legitimate question, but it is not reason enough to deny the obvious—that there was indeed a Creator. The evidence to this fact is so overwhelming that one has to have seriously flawed reasoning to deny it—or to be as Paul declared, **"darkened in their understanding."**

Discovering the marvels of the creation is wonderful, but even much more marvelous is that the Creator actually loves us and wants to have a relationship with us! In fact, He created us for that purpose. Any knowledge, wisdom, or philosophy that does not lead us closer to God is working contrary to the very purpose for which man was created, and which alone can satisfy the deepest longing of his soul.

Of course, the issue of the Creator has obviously been settled for those of you who are reading this. So what can we do to help those who are in the grip of a **"darkened"** understanding? The most effective thing that we can do to help those who are in such a deep delusion is to walk in what we have been called to—fellowship with the Son. Let us persevere and encourage one another to excel more and more in doing that which gives our great God His greatest pleasure. As Paul wrote in I Corinthians 1:4-9:

> **I thank my God always concerning you, for the grace of God which was given you in Christ Jesus,**
>
> **that in everything you were enriched in Him, in all speech and all knowledge,**
>
> **even as the testimony concerning Christ was confirmed in you,**
>
> **so that you are not lacking in any gift, awaiting eagerly the revelation of our Lord Jesus Christ,**

who shall also confirm you to the end, blameless in the day of our Lord Jesus Christ.

God is faithful, through whom you were called into fellowship with His Son, Jesus Christ our Lord.

My point is that those who are so darkened in their understanding and futile in their reasoning are rarely going to be reached with reasoning. However, there is nothing on this earth more contagious than a person who is getting closer to God. They will manifest and lift up Jesus in all that they do, and when He is lifted up, all will be drawn to Him.

There has been an age-old debate as to whether we must understand in order to believe, or believe in order to understand. Both are true to a degree, but the latter normally precedes the former. The devil has put a veil over people's eyes that they cannot see through without the help of the Holy Spirit. With the help of the Holy Spirit, any veil that the devil has placed can be easily penetrated.

I personally have enjoyed reading the works of Einstein, Stephen W. Hawking, and others. These great thinkers are not so foolish as to deny God, but simply want to know how He did what He did. In some of Einstein's writings it seems as if he clearly perceived the Word of God as John described Him in the first chapter of his gospel. Only Einstein did not know that He had been made flesh and had walked among us. Paul was right in the first chapter of Romans when he said that the Lord is clearly seen in the things that were made.

Even so, the point of knowing that there is a God is not enough. We must go on to know why He created us, and how He wants to relate to us. This must begin with the restoration of our relationship with Him which can only come through the cross. The atonement also means at-one-ment, or the way that we are re-unified. Just knowing that God exists, without having a restored relationship with Him, still leaves us in futility and darkness.

CHAPTER THIRTY-SEVEN

Renewing Our Minds

In the next verses of our study, we are told how we are to rise above futile thinking to begin renewing our minds so that all darkness and futility is removed, which is stated in Ephesians 4:20-24:

> **But you did not learn Christ in this way,**
>
> **if indeed you have heard Him and have been taught in Him, just as truth is in Jesus,**
>
> **that, in reference to your former manner of life, you lay aside the old self, which is being corrupted in accordance with the lusts of deceit,**
>
> **and that you be renewed in the spirit of your mind,**
>
> **and put on the new self, which in the likeness of God has been created in righteousness and holiness of the truth.**

Those who **"learn Christ"** will be lovers of truth, righteousness and holiness just as He is. Such things are preliminary to any real knowledge about the universe. The universe was actually created in truth and righteousness, and the corruption and discord in it is only because of the Fall.

So, is this "renewing of our minds" taking place in the church? Studies show that there has been a veritable meltdown of morality and integrity in the church over the last three decades. In general, the church has actually been going in the opposite direction with Christians becoming more conformed to the image of the world, or even the devil, than to the image of Christ. Few shepherds seem to be doing anything about it, and many of those who claim to be watchmen have spent more time attacking other Christians than sounding the alarm. Western Christianity may now be in its most grave crisis.

Christians should be the most free and creative people on earth. No one should be more creative than those who know the Creator and are being changed into His image. Yet, why does the church tend to be so boringly uniform and devoid of creativity? Many of the popular trends in the church are just weak copies of trends in the world, only a couple of decades behind the world, and poorly done. Why? This also reflects a void of the life of the Creator in our midst.

This great tragedy of Christianity is primarily a result of the religious spirit dominating much of the church, substituting religious performance for true **"righteousness and holiness of the truth."** The religious spirit is empowered by the fear of man, which compels us to seek the approval and acceptance of other men, rather than to grow in a true relationship with our God. In this way it becomes a substitute for the way that we are to be **"renewed in the spirit of our mind."** To be renewed means to think new—to think differently. You can't do that if you are overly concerned about what others think of you.

We must beware of the anti-Christ spirit that is seeking to dominate the world at the end of the age, which is primarily a substitute for Christ. It actually takes its seat in the temple of God, which is the church, proclaiming itself to be the Christ or the anointed. There is a false anointing that is taking its seat in the church which we must discern. It is the spirit of the world and is devoted to worldliness in place of true holiness.

True holiness is the result of our beholding the glory of the Lord and being changed into His image from glory to glory. It is a renewing process in which we gradually begin to see and think differently than those who are worldly-minded. We must

174

understand that some of the most worldly-minded are religious people who have a relationship to a religion instead of to a living God.

True holiness is based on our relationship to God, it is not just trying to figure out and comply with the rules written in the Book. The New Testament was not intended to be another Law. There are commandments that we must obey, and there are guidelines that will keep us on course, but these are given to set us free to be who God created us to be. However, this freedom is not an opportunity for the flesh, but it is freedom to choose righteousness and holiness because that is who we are.

To grow in the true holiness of God releases the true nobility and glory of God's highest creation on the earth—man. There is a "beauty of holiness" that exudes such a dignity and grace that when anyone beholds it, they will be struck with how it is the very nature that they too were created to be. True holiness is not based on religious performance, but on beholding the dignity and glory of that which is so far above earthly, carnal, behavior, that it makes all other endeavors pale in comparison.

True holiness is a strong foundation which will also give us the confidence to be truly creative, but not try to be different for the purpose of getting the attention of other people. Creativity for the purpose of gaining attention will always be shallow. The creativity that comes from knowing the Creator will have the signature of heaven on it.

Before the end of this age the Lord will have a bride who is pure and without spot or wrinkle. She will not attain this because of fear or out of religious performance, but because of such a burning love for her Lord that she is consumed with doing all things to please Him. This bride is being prepared now, right at the time when the deepest darkness is starting to cover the earth, and because of this darkness, her light will shine even brighter. All of creation will, for all time, declare that those who persevered to be a part of the glorious church which will emerge and stand against the greatest darkness, are worthy to rule with Him. You are called to be a part of this bride. Do you have anything better to do?

CHAPTER THIRTY-EIGHT

Loving the Truth

Our text for this chapter is Ephesians 4:25:

Therefore, laying aside falsehood, speak truth, each one of you, with his neighbor, for we are members of one another.

When we think of truth and error we often relate it to doctrinal truth and error. Doctrinal truth is of course important, but walking in truth requires far more than just doctrinal truth. We can know all doctrines accurately, but if we are prone to deception and cheating in our relationships with others, we are walking in deception and promoting the kingdom of darkness instead of the kingdom of God.

One of the most basic contrasts between the kingdom of God and the kingdom of darkness is that the kingdom of God is built upon truth, but the power of the evil one is deception. Therefore, the more firmly we are established in the kingdom of God, the more devoted to truth we will be. Likewise, every deception that we allow to remain in our lives will be an open door for the evil one to enter our lives.

Because this present world is so full of deception, one of the greatest treasures we can have is truth. Another of the greatest gifts we can have, which will help us navigate through this life, is the ability to discern truth from lies. Seeking truth, and the discernment for distinguishing truth, should therefore be a basic devotion of every Christian. The foundation for this is our own devotion to truth without compromise in our own lives.

As we are told in II Thessalonians 2:10, it is not those who have truth who are not deceived in the last days, but those who have **"the love of the truth."** There can be a big difference between having truth and loving it. We can want truth, even doctrinal truth for many evil reasons, such as just to prove our own positions or to attack churches or others who may have some doctrinal error. Those who have a sincere love of the truth should also walk in love when they use the truth. Only then will we use the truth that we have been entrusted with to help set others free, not to attack them.

One deception we have seen which frequently seduces people is the lie that if they are doing things which are not in their heart then they are hypocrites. Many have fallen into drug use or illicit sex because they feel that they are not following their true heart if they do not follow through with their desires. This may seem foolish to some, but deception is very deceptive, and many fall to this kind of foolishness. However, to fall in this way reveals that one is not really a lover of the truth. The truth is that none of us are a lover of truth unless the Lord helps us.

When Adam and Eve tried to hide after the Fall, it revealed the tendency to run from the truth. When they were found they did not seek truth, they sought to shift the blame for their sin, which is fallen man's nature. However, we must keep in mind that God does not forgive excuses—He forgives sin when it is acknowledged. A life devoted to truth begins with acknowledging our own transgressions and mistakes. If we are still trying to hide them, or shift the blame for them, we are not yet lovers of truth.

We are not being an "honest" person by doing what is "in our heart" when we are drawn into sin—we are being a carnal, sinful person. Doing what we feel is not how we walk in truth, but how we walk in the evil, fallen nature that denies Christ. Truth is not a feeling—truth is a Person. Jesus is the Truth. Walking in truth is abiding in Him. Would Jesus do the things we feel compelled to do?

He prayed in John 17:17, **"Sanctify them in the truth; Thy word is truth."** Following carnal desires because it is what we desire to do is not being true to ourselves, but is submitting to the ultimate lie, the very one that deceived Eve. This is not an issue of whether we are being true to who we really are as much as it is whether we are going to live by the flesh or the Spirit, as we are told in Romans 8:5-9:

> **For those who are according to the flesh set their minds on the things of the flesh, but those who are according to the Spirit, the things of the Spirit.**
>
> **For the mind set on the flesh is death, but the mind set on the Spirit is life and peace,**
>
> **because the mind set on the flesh is hostile toward God; for it does not subject itself to the law of God, for it is not even able to do so;**
>
> **and those who are in the flesh cannot please God.**
>
> **However, you are not in the flesh but in the Spirit, if indeed the Spirit of God dwells in you. But if anyone does not have the Spirit of Christ, he does not belong to Him.**

To walk in truth we must **"deny ourselves,"** or our fallen, carnal natures, crucify them, and determine that obedience to God and pleasing Him is more important to us than any other personal gratification that we could have. In John 14:6 Jesus said, **"I am the way, and the truth, and the life; no one comes to the Father, but through Me."** In John 4:23-24 He says, **"But an hour is coming, and now is, when the true worshipers shall worship the Father in spirit and truth; for such people the Father seeks to be His worshipers. God is spirit, and those who worship Him must worship in spirit and truth."**

As our text for this chapter exhorts us to **"lay aside all falsehood,"** this begins with us laying aside our tendency to deceive ourselves by trying to justify that which is clearly forbidden by the Scriptures, and is a violation of the Spirit of God who lives in us. As John 3:21 states, **"But he who practices the truth comes to the light, that his deeds may be manifested as having been wrought in God."**

In John 8:32 we are told, **"...and you shall know the truth, and the truth shall make you free."** The truth is that you were created too noble and too exalted as a child of the most high God to continue submitting yourself to the base lies of the enemy and to obey him rather than the King to whom you have given your life and body.

Now let us look at the next two verses in our study for another application of this, Ephesians 4:26-27:

> **Be angry, and yet do not sin; do not let the sun go down on your anger,**
>
> **and do not give the devil an opportunity.**

This raises a good question. Can we be angry and not sin? The answer is "yes." We are called to be like the Lord, and to abide in Him, and He very definitely gets angry at some things, so it is to be expected that we too can have righteous anger.

This should cause us to want to understand what those things are that make the Lord angry. Some of them are injustice, unrighteousness, perversion, and taking advantage of the weak. A study of the anger of the Lord is important for every Christian. If you do this you will also find some things that make Him angry that will probably surprise you.

For example, the anger of the Lord **"burned against Moses" (Exodus 4:14)** when the Lord called him to go to Egypt to set His people free and Moses responded by saying that he was not adequate for such a great task. This may seem like humility, and since the Lord promises to give His grace to the humble it is hard to understand why He would get angry at Moses for this. However, this is not true humility, but rather a profound arrogance. What Moses was really saying by this response was that he did not think the Lord knew what He was doing by choosing him. Moses was also saying by this response that the Lord's adequacy was not as great as Moses' inadequacy.

The obvious truth was that Moses was indeed inadequate for the task. So are every one of us with anything the Lord calls us to do. If we were adequate within ourselves we would not need

Him. The type of false humility that Moses demonstrated can therefore be the basis for the most destructive kind of pride in leadership. The same logic presupposes that those the Lord chooses must be adequate in themselves. This is also the root of humanism that supposes that mankind has both the wisdom and goodness to do what is right—a remarkable delusion in the light of human history.

So there is righteous anger, but we are exhorted not to let the sun go down on our anger. This means that we should settle such matters before we go to bed, and should be a rule in every relationship. Even when the Lord's anger burned against Moses, He settled the matter immediately. The Lord also did not reject Moses because of his folly. Even those who are doing and promoting the most unrighteous deeds which God hates are still loved by Him. The Lord even said that He gave Jezebel time to repent (see Revelation 2:20-21). He truly does desire for all to repent and be saved. Even so, He is still angry at our sins.

We must also consider that the exhortation in the verse above is a warning that when you are angry you are in danger of sinning. Certainly some of the worst crimes and diabolical deeds in history have been the result of uncontrolled anger. This is such an important issue that when Paul gave Titus the qualifications for those who would be elders in the church he said: **"For the overseer must be above reproach as God's steward, not self-willed, not quick-tempered" (Titus 1:7)**. Being **"quick tempered"** therefore disqualifies one from being a leader in the church. This is because to **"be angry, and yet do not sin"** means that we may get angry, but we do not let the anger control us, we control it.

Two of the Lord's future great apostles also wanted to call fire down on people who rejected the Lord. The Lord rebuked them saying that they did not know of what spirit they were. The Lord even forgave the ones who crucified Him, asking the Father not to hold it against them. There is a righteous anger, but it is not selfish. It does not rise because we are offended or rejected, but because people are hurt, deceived, and seduced by evil. Those who are not mature enough to control the anger generated by offenses or rejection are not mature enough to be in leadership in the church. This sin of unrighteous anger hurts many people, and it is a departure from the truth of God's nature and ways. If we love the truth, we will also love all of the fruits of the Spirit, including peace and patience.

In the next verse in our study, Ephesians 4:28, Paul is further establishing the ways that are based on the truth of God's ways:

Let him who steals steal no longer; but rather let him labor, performing with his own hands what is good, in order that he may have something to share with him who has need.

CHAPTER THIRTY-NINE

Labor or Steal

"**Thou shalt not steal**" (**Exodus 20:15** KJV) is one of the Ten Commandments that was to be the foundation of God's standard for righteousness, or the right way that we should live. Stealing is contrary to the nature of God because it is in basic conflict with justice and fairness. The counterpoint to stealing is not only laboring for what we need, but also having something to give to those in need. That's because truth is abiding in the Truth, Himself, and He came to give because He is also love. Therefore, our devotion to labor is for more than just "making a living," but is to have something to help others with.

As we have covered previously, man was created to have fellowship with God, and to cultivate the garden and rule over it. We might basically say that we were created for fellowship and labor. It is therefore understandable that studies have revealed that anyone who is not engaged in meaningful labor will go insane. We were created to have meaningful labor in our life and if that is denied, it will affect the very core of our identity as human beings.

We might also carry this a little further and consider that it is only to the degree we are engaged in meaningful labor that we can be fulfilled and at peace within ourselves. The ultimate and most meaningful labor is that which we do in ministry, performing our functions as members of the body of Christ. We should also consider that the most "meaningful" labor is that which is done for the most noble purpose—giving unselfishly to others.

"Meaningful" does not necessarily imply that it is labor that we enjoy or want to do either. Our fulfillment does not always come from the task itself, but from knowing that we have accomplished something which needs to be done. Even so, the curse that came upon man after the Fall was **"toil" (Genesis 3:17),** which is labor accomplished "with great or painful effort." The curse was not labor, but labor that was unnecessarily difficult for the results produced. Many who faithfully labor for their means are still under this curse, having to labor far too much for the results achieved. One of the benefits achieved for us by the cross of Jesus was the removal of every curse including the curse of toil. How is this achieved?

We might tend to think that this will be achieved by getting a better job, higher pay for our work, etc., but that is not necessarily so. When I first became a Christian I took a construction job that was pure drudgery. Not only was it hard labor, it was dirty and hot, and paid very little in the beginning as I was just a common laborer. Then I decided that I was going to do my job as unto the Lord, considering that everything I was involved in building was for the Lord Himself to occupy. Very soon my job became so fulfilling that I could not wait to get to the job each morning. I also became known for having an uncommon devotion to excellence in every job that I was given. This caused my employers to invest in my training, helping me to advance, receiving faster than normal promotions. In less than two years I was paid as a full journeyman carpenter. This was a non-union job, but the company I was working for was one that had never advanced anyone this far in less than four years, and it often took six. I was not better or smarter than the others, but I advanced because of my attitude. Even more importantly, I lived with a tremendous sense of accomplishment and fulfillment from my job.

Our goal should not be to remove the labor, but to remove the curse that is on it so that our labor is productive and fulfilling.

The most basic way this is done is by turning every task into worship, doing everything as unto the Lord. Another way the curse is removed may surprise us.

Most people go to work to provide for themselves and their families. This is certainly a good reason for labor, but it is not the one which we are exhorted to have in our verse for this chapter. We are told to labor in order to have something to share with those who have need. That is Christian love. Doing things for others is actually one of the most fulfilling things we can do, and is the reason why so many who do not even know the Lord become philanthropists. There is a remarkable satisfaction in giving.

There are some who cannot labor. The Lord also said we would have the poor with us always. There are certainly some who are poor because of laziness or irresponsibility, but most of the world's poor are simply born into conditions that make anything other than a life of poverty nearly impossible. James also said that God chose the poor of this world to be rich in faith (see James 2:5). We should never look down on the poor, but rather consider it an honor and privilege to serve those who are called to be rich in faith.

We must also consider that many of the jobs which have become the least esteemed, such as being a housewife and mother devoted to raising children, are some of the most important jobs on earth. Every mother in Christ is a "queen mother," given the unfathomable honor of raising the future kings and queens who will rule over the earth. What could be more important than that? They may not derive a direct wage for this task, but who could ever put a value on it? Why would anyone want to give that position up for a mere earthly profession? I am certainly not against women having professions, but we must always keep first things first, and our jobs as parents are a much greater honor and responsibility, and can be much more fulfilling, than any other jobs we can have. In my opinion, the men are called mainly to be the providers so that the women can stay home and do the really important things, which have more honor. What gives any parent more honor than great children?

We must always remember that the true purpose for our labor is to be a blessing to others. When our job is done for this reason it will cease to be toil and become a glorious and fulfilling act of worship.

CHAPTER FORTY

Words That Build

There are few things that would more radically affect our life for good than obedience to the next verse in our study, Ephesians 4:29:

> **Let no unwholesome word proceed from your mouth, but only such a word as is good for edification according to the need of the moment, that it may give grace to those who hear.**

We briefly addressed this verse previously but it is worthy of a much more in-depth look. Consider how different life would be if all of our words were used to build up instead of tear down, to impart faith and hope instead of doubt, and love and peace instead of fear and division. This one thing could transform the church from the babel of confusion that it now is to the most extraordinary, wonderful, and powerful family that it is called to be.

Proverbs 18:21 states, **"Death and life are in the power of the tongue."** How could such a small member of our body have such power? Words are actually the most powerful force on earth, controlling the destiny of nations much more surely than armies or politics ever have. That is why James wrote that **"... if anyone does not stumble in what he says, he is a perfect man, able to bridle the whole body as well" (James 3:2).** Ponder that for just a little while—if we can control our tongues we will be perfect, able to control our whole body as well! This is because, as we are told in Matthew 12:34, **"For the mouth speaks out of that which fills the heart."** Therefore, if our mouth is only speaking that which is pure, it is because it is pure. This is confirmed in James 3:3-8:

> **Now if we put the bits into the horses' mouths so that they may obey us, we direct their entire body as well.**
>
> **Behold, the ships also, though they are so great and are driven by strong winds, are still directed by a very small rudder, wherever the inclination of the pilot desires.**
>
> **So also the tongue is a small part of the body, and yet it boasts of great things. Behold, how great a forest is set aflame by such a small fire!**
>
> **And the tongue is a fire, the very world of iniquity; the tongue is set among our members as that which defiles the entire body, and sets on fire the course of our life, and is set on fire by hell.**
>
> **For every species of beasts and birds, of reptiles and creatures of the sea, is tamed, and has been tamed by the human race.**
>
> **But no one can tame the tongue; it is a restless evil and full of deadly poison.**

If it is true as stated here that our tongues actually set the course of our life, how much more devoted should we be to our tongues giving life instead of death, faith and hope instead of doubt and hopelessness, and love and peace instead of bitterness and division? We must also remember as we are told in Galatians 6:7, **"Do not be deceived, God is not mocked; for whatever a man sows, this he will also reap."** Therefore, if we want to reap life and faith we need to sow life and faith. If we want to reap grace and mercy we need to sow grace and mercy. However, if we are sowing bitterness and division, these things will come back to us. With our words we are sowing what we are going to reap.

This is why one of the most important things we can do in our lives is to learn to control what we say, speaking only those things which edify and build others up, determining that we will **"let no unwholesome word proceed from our mouths..."**

One way we can begin to control our words, and start setting a more positive course for our lives, is to do a word fast. Fasting is one of the biblical ways that we can humble ourselves; and God gives His grace to the humble. A word fast is when we determine to reduce our communication to just what is absolutely essential to perform our jobs or other essential duties. Like fasting from food, it is probably advisable that you start with a short fast, and then work up to longer ones. Not only will this help you to control what comes out of your mouth, but you will also have the added benefit of God giving His grace to you.

One of the goals of a word fast could be to reduce the number of words we speak at all times by 50 percent. If you do this you will be amazed at how much more others will start to respect you, perceiving you to be one of greater wisdom, as we are told in the following verses:

> **"When there are many words, transgression is unavoidable, but he who restrains his lips is wise (Proverbs 10:19).**

> **"He who restrains his words has knowledge, and he who has a cool spirit is a man of understanding." Even a fool, when he keeps silent, is considered wise; when he closes his lips, he is counted prudent (Proverbs 17:27-28).**

When we start to gain control of our words, we will treat each word like precious ammunition which we want to carefully use to hit the target in order to edify others. We may only speak 10 percent as much as we used to, but we will bear much more good fruit. The ones who learn to control their tongues are also the ones who can be trusted with the greatest prophetic anointing because they are not "loose cannons," but they know how to hit the target with words that have prophetic power.

CHAPTER FORTY-ONE

Do Not Grieve the Spirit

Our text for this chapter is Ephesians 4:30-32:

And do not grieve the Holy Spirit of God, by whom you were sealed for the day of redemption.

Let all bitterness and wrath and anger and clamor and slander be put away from you, along with all malice.

And be kind to one another, tender-hearted, forgiving each other, just as God in Christ also has forgiven you.

As we are temples of the Holy Spirit, one of the primary endeavors of our life should be to learn how we could be proper hosts of the Holy Spirit. What is it that blesses and pleases Him? What is it that grieves Him?

Certainly we should all make a supreme effort to **"not grieve the Holy Spirit,"** but it seems that few people connect with how we actually do this. In fact, almost every exhortation I have ever heard about what grieves the Spirit has been how people tend to interrupt what He wants to do. Somehow I don't think this grieves Him very much. After all, is patience not one of the primary fruits of the Spirit? Certainly He has enough patience to not be grieved at mere interruptions. We are told in the verses above what grieves Him—bitterness, wrath, anger, clamor, slander, or malice. To the degree that these remain in our lives we are making His home within us uncomfortable at best.

"**Bitterness**" is basically unforgiveness. Wrath is retaliation for wrongs or perceived wrongs. "**Anger**" is basic selfishness which is usually the result of feeling that our rights or interests were somehow violated. "**Clamor**" is the disturbance that we cause by the agitation of our souls which is the result of all of the above. "**Slander**" is simply uniting with the devil, the "**accuser of the brethren**" (**Revelation 12:10**), to do his evil to God's people. "**Malice**" is the result of the devil having a deep root of evil, which he is able to maintain in our soul. By maintaining these things in our lives, we are actually being a better host to the devil than we are to the Spirit.

I know as a father one of the things that irritates me the most is when my children fight with each other. Likewise, one of the things that blesses me the most is when they are tender-hearted, forgiving each other, and getting along. As we are told in Proverbs 21:9, "**It is better to live in a corner of a roof than in a house shared with a contentious woman.**" Do you think this "**contentious woman**" could be the bride of Christ, and that the Holy Spirit would rather live somewhere else until we learn to get along? After all, this Scripture too was inspired by the Spirit.

Good teaching and preaching are important for the health of any church, but one moment of the manifest presence of the Lord can accomplish more than many years of just teaching. If we are in pursuit of genuine New Testament church life as it is intended, our number one devotion should be to be the place in which the Lord loves to dwell. This is true whether we want Him to dwell in our homes or in our services. Therefore, if we are not going to grieve Him, we must put away all bitterness, wrath, anger, clamor, slander, or malice. If we are going to bless Him, we will have to start loving and forgiving one another.

Of course, it is good to not want to grieve the Spirit, but we should want to go further than that and be the best hosts for Him that we can possibly be. This should compel us to study the places and people that He used in Scripture, conforming our lives to be like those that He obviously chose to use and abide in. We could never have a better companion than the Holy Spirit. Wouldn't it be great if He said that about us? This is worthy of anyone's life pursuit.